If you long to live out a faith that shines with purpose, meaning, and fruitfulness, read *Significant*! Carol McLeod writes with biblical wisdom, personal transparency, and a passion for equipping you to know how significant you are to God, how important your life's work is, and how you can make a lasting impact on others. This book will inspire and prepare you to embrace God's design for your life and to know, beyond any doubt, how much you are loved by Him. Read it first for yourself and then gather your friends together and use *Significant* as a small group study.

—*Carol Kent*
Speaker and author, *Becoming a Woman of Influence*

Once again, my dear friend Carol McLeod masterfully motivates with truth, wisdom, and insights, which her years of life, motherhood, and service have given her. She knows the way and compels us to follow, finding deeper meaning and joy than we thought were possible. Her gift is a gift to the world!

—*Lynette Lewis*
Author, speaker, business consultant, TEDx presenter, and pastor's wife

Significant is perhaps the most powerful of all Carol McLeod's books. It is Carol at her best. Prepare to be moved out of your comfort zone and into your destiny zone. God has big plans for you, as Carol shows with this powerful statement: "I believe that, as a woman filled with the power of the Holy Spirit and armed with the plans of God, you should actually do *more* of what scares you!" I believe every woman in today's generation needs to read this book!

—*Becky Harling*
International conference speaker
Author, *Who Do You Say That I Am?* and *How to Listen so People Will Talk*

This book will speak to everyone who reads it! We are bombarded with multiple opportunities to feel inadequate and irrelevant when it comes to being a wife, mother, friend, employee, or significant other. We get lost in the caretaker role and completely forget that we are children of God who are loved unconditionally and have a divine purpose. God is with us and for us, and *Significant* will help you understand the depths of God's love for you. By applying Scripture to everyday challenges, Carol has a unique gift in sharing what so many of us feel. This book is a life changer!

—*Robbie Raugh*, RN/Nutritionist
Author, *The Raw Truth Recharge: 7 Truths for Total Health and Fitness*
Host, *The Raw Truth with Robbie Raugh*, ESPN Radio, WDCX radio
Cohost, *The Keri and Robbie Show*, WDCX radio

I wish I'd had this book in hand when my wife and I were raising our two daughters, now in their twenties. While addressing the early years of innocent discovery, the teen years of "Who am I?" and the adult years of "What's my purpose?" *Significant* details a striking contrast between a woman who determines her worth through the eyes of the world and one who rises above that distorted outlook to identify herself as who she is in Christ. Carol and I go back to our college days together, and what she has written is a treasure of insight into how God has created every woman for a significant life—a life with eternal purpose. This message is vital for women in today's culture who are battling the busyness and stress of daily life and need to be grounded in a biblical understanding of who they are. You can bet I'll be getting copies for my wife and daughters.

—*Clay Jacobsen*
Author of four Christian novels
Director, *Jeopardy!* television program

Wow, this new book by Carol McLeod, *Significant: Becoming a Woman of Unique Purpose, True Identity, and Irrepressible Hope*, will challenge every woman's paradigm about finding identity in Christ! Carol reminds us, emphatically, that if you don't discover you are known by God, you will always be looking to be known by something or someone else. And you will never be satisfied. I know this book's target is women, but I have personally been blessed and helped by Carol's words. My first copy of this book goes to my wife.

—*Tim Cameron*
Educator and speaker
Author, *The Forty-Day Word Fast*
Husband of forty-eight years

God has given Carol a timely and powerful message for every woman who will be brave enough to pick up this book and read it. Do you feel invisible to God? Are you struggling with a sense of smallness? The truth is, the King of creation has ordained you to represent Him on the earth with a sound no one else can make. As you read *Significant*, you will realize afresh that through your unique, God-given personality, you have been carefully selected to personify the royal heart of God for the person in front of you. In *Significant*, Carol uncovers what the enemy has hidden from you. When you truly know who you are and that royal blood flows through your veins—there is no demon in hell that will be able to stop you. *Significant* will effectively assist you with how to clothe yourself with your God-given identity.

—*Christy Christopher*
Speaker and author, *Until the Day Breaks and the Shadows Flee* and
Incredible Intervention

Carol McLeod has done it again. *Significant* is power-packed with God's purpose, passion, and plans for every woman of God on the planet. I was moved to tears when I read the line, "History would be incomplete without your biography." WHAT IF we lived our lives with that message at the base of our understanding? Thank you, Carol, for sharing from the heart of God in this new book. The seeds planted with these words will produce greatness in those who read and embrace them.

—*Johnie Hampton*
CEO, Hampton Creative, Tulsa, OK

Significant by Carol McLeod is delightfully exhilarating and appropriately sobering. In this new book, Carol comes beside us and reminds us that our significance as women doesn't come from beauty, brains, or talent, but from how God created us for His glorious purposes and plans. Yet sometimes those purposes come through pain and heartache, and Carol holds our hands and shows us how God often does His best work through difficulties. You will come away from *Significant* encouraged, emboldened, and empowered.

—*Sarah Sundin*
Best-selling and award-winning author of *The Sea Before Us* and
The Sky Above Us

In *Significant*, Carol McLeod encourages us, as today's women of faith, to put aside the lies that negate our self-confidence and ministry, and to find our true significance in God. She exposes the misconceptions we've believed for so long and gently leads us to this beautiful truth: we are here to reveal the story of Jesus. Sisters, do not miss this amazing message of inspiration and hope.

—*Kim de Blecourt*
Author, *Until We All Come Home* and *I Call You Mine*

Have you ever read Jeremiah 29:11 and wondered if those plans and purposes of God were for everyone but you? By the end of Carol McLeod's book *Significant*, you will know with certainty that you personally matter to God. This new confidence of purpose and partnership with the Holy Spirit will motivate you to fulfill God's plans for you to influence the world. The power of *Significant* comes from two sources. The first is the living Word of God itself, which is masterfully unpacked on every page. The second flows from the life of the author herself, who determined early in her walk with God to courageously live the Word, day in and day out, not just teach it. Encountering God and His daughter Carol will change your life, I promise!

—*Faith Blatchford*
Author, speaker, and creativity consultant
www.faithblatchford.com

Many books have broached the subject of significance and its endless pursuit by humans. In her eleventh book (a significant achievement itself), Carol McLeod explores a different tack on the subject from the perspective of a woman who has nurtured a deep relationship with God and Scripture. I keep recommending Carol's books because they keep getting even better. This one will touch you deeply as you explore not only the Bible, but also Carol's amazing personal story of finding her place of significance and value in life. A treasure awaits. Dig here.

—*Chris Busch*
Founder and CEO, LightQuest Media, Inc.

You might not think that the world needs you, but it does. God planned it that way. Carol McLeod's new book, *Significant*, speaks to the most profound truth inside each one of us—our reason for living. This book is important because it reveals that the Lord has connected people to you who are waiting to be shown His love. You may be the response to their prayer. A solution to their problem. An answer to their question. An introduction to Jesus and an invitation to eternal life! No one can speak with your voice, say your words, smile your smile, or shine your light. No one can take your place; it is yours alone to fill. You are destined to impact the world around you in a significant way. This masterful book reveals God's desire for you to be exactly what He made you to be and to live the story no one else can live—the story of your own significant life.

—*John Mason*
Author, *An Enemy Called Average* and many other best sellers

If Carol lived any closer to me, a private lunch with her would be on my weekly schedule! She is the mentor women my age need and the friend every woman wants. Carol's willingness to be vulnerable with her longings for significance flow from a security she has in knowing God's good nature. She reminds us that what we long for matters, both to God and for our story! She points us to Him with her every word and models for us how we can experience the same security and peace for ourselves.

—*Heather DeJesus Yates*
Best-selling author, *All the Wild Pearls: A Guide for Passing Down Redemptive Stories*
and *A Mother of Thousands: From Barren to Revolutionary*

The Bible confirms, through its many examples of courageous women, that God's call and anointing are not limited to only one gender. In her Scripture-soaked book *Significance*, Carol McLeod empowers every woman to boldly pursue, and then fully embrace, her God-ordained purpose.

—*Marty Nystrom*
Author and composer, "As the Deer" and over 120 other worship songs

Girlfriends, God has assigned a mission just for us—but we must choose to accept it. That sounds simple, but it's so easy to become caught up in our fears and all the "But, what if…?" questions that our mission is over before it even begins. That's why I'm so excited about Carol McLeod's new book, *Significant*. Carol shares encouragement and wisdom to help us find and fulfill the purpose God has for our lives—becoming women of significance for Him.

—*Michelle Cox*
Coauthor, *Just 18 Summers* and *When God Calls the Heart* devotional series

Who am I? Why was I created? What is my purpose? Mankind has asked these questions for centuries, trying to determine how to live a life of significance. To find answers, speaker and teacher Carol McLeod has explored God's Word and gleaned truths from the One who created us. In her new book, *Significant*, she uses personal stories and biblical insights to lead us into a deeper understanding of who God says we are and why we were created. Through years of joy, pain, parenting, teaching, and serving, Carol knows firsthand what it means to be a woman of significance, and she freely shares her wisdom with us. By reading this book, you too will be inspired to lead a life of *significance*!

—*Melissa G. Bolden*
Pastor, author, speaker, and teacher
MBolden Ministry

Carol clearly understands the pulse of women in this generation. She speaks with authority and sensitivity to every woman—just like me—who longs to walk confidently in her God-given purpose. Her keen insights and scriptural context move us from the frustration of craving significance to the fulfillment of fleshing out our calling.

—*Angela Donadio*
Speaker and author, *Finding Joy When Life Is Out of Focus: Philippians—A Study for Joy-Thirsty Women* and
Fearless: Ordinary Women of the Bible Who Dared to Do Extraordinary Things

CAROL M^cLEOD

SIGNIFICANT

BECOMING A WOMAN OF UNIQUE PURPOSE, TRUE IDENTITY, AND IRREPRESSIBLE HOPE

WHITAKER
HOUSE

SIGNIFICANT:
Becoming a Woman of Unique Purpose, True Identity, and Irrepressible Hope

Carol Burton McLeod
carol@carolmcleodministries.com
www.carolmcleodministries.com
Carol McLeod Ministries ✦ PO Box 1274 ✦ Orchard Park, NY 14127 ✦ 855-569-5433

ISBN: 978-1-64123-306-4 ✦ eBook ISBN: 978-1-64123-307-1
Printed in the United States of America
© 2019 by Carol Burton McLeod

Whitaker House ✦ 1030 Hunt Valley Circle ✦ New Kensington, PA 15068
www.whitakerhouse.com

Library of Congress Control Number: 2019947930

1 2 3 4 5 6 7 8 9 10 11 ⊔⊔ 26 25 24 23 22 21 20 19

Contents

Foreword by Amy Groeschel 15

A Personal Word from Carol.. 19

Introduction: The Search for Significance 23

Part One: *You Are...a Woman!*

1. The Wonder of YOU!... 31

2. It's Time... 37

3. A Few Good Women.. 43

Part Two: *You Are...a Woman of Unmatched Purpose*

4. On Purpose…for Purpose…with Purpose........................ 49

5. Plans? What Plans?... 55

6. One Thousand Years Later 63

7. "I Knew You" 69

8. I Didn't Sign Up for the Battles! 79

9. When the Hard Stuff Becomes the Good Stuff................. 85

10. Joe and I......93

11. He Needed One of You......99

Part Three: *You Are...a Woman of Glorious Identity*

12. Nice to Meet You, Self!......111

13. The "Muchness" of You......117

14. More to Your Story......127

15. No Shame......133

16. Who Told You?......141

17. You Are More Than Enough......149

18. Your Name Is.........155

19. You Are Who He Says You Are......163

Part Four: *You Are...Never Alone*

20. The Loneliest Number?......175

21. Jesus with Skin On......185

22. A Season of Ice-Cold Loneliness......191

23. Just like Jesus!......199

Part Five: *You Are...a Woman of Grace and Peace*

24. Can a Woman "Have It All"?......209

25. Overwhelmed......217

26. Today, Not Tomorrow......221

27. The Stuff of Which Eternity Is Made......229

28. There Is a Place......237

Epilogue: You Are...Significant!......247

Acknowledgments......251

About the Author......256

Foreword

"I want you to hear and know that God is pleased with you. He has more for you to do for His glory. Do not give up or grow weary from disappointments. Trust His plans for you."

These words are a paraphrase of the life-giving encouragement I received from Carol McLeod. We had met just moments earlier. My amazing mother had arranged for us to get together, believing Carol and I would enjoy knowing each other. I soon discovered Carol to be a deep well of joy, wisdom, and humble love. I never expected to receive such direct and heartfelt encouragement from her that day. She refreshed my anxious heart. It was clear that her radiant, demonstrative love came from a long and intimate walk with God. Along her journey, Carol has learned and lived a truth we all need to embrace: our significance comes from God.

If someone were to look at my life from a distance, they might be fooled into thinking that it is nearly perfect. And actually, it is pretty wonderful. I have a very good marriage. That alone seems to be a rarity nowadays. Our six children—and two grandchildren at present—are all accounted for and seem to love us (their folks) and our Savior. My husband, Craig, and I founded and lead a thriving church. I direct a healthy and growing housing program for women who are in transition. My life is truly good. Still, with all these notable blessings, I often battle with self-doubt and feelings of insignificance, asking myself questions such as these:

"Does what I do really make a difference? Or, am I just wasting my time?"

"What if I fail at preparing my kids for their futures?"

"Am I holding the ministry back by not being an effective enough leader?"

"Why do 'they' always seem to do 'it' better than I do?"

"I am just average at everything. How can God truly use 'average'"?

Whether your life is mostly mundane and seemingly insignificant, or filled with ongoing adventure and sensational successes, I bet insecurity and personal disappointment try to pull you down, too. The dangerous lies of self-doubt are poisonous arrows that linger long in the soul, with great potential for stunting our effectiveness.

You may ask yourself, "Am I important? Does what I do from day to day matter?" Though it may be tempting to do so, don't look to social media posts to find the answers to these questions. Your life is far greater and more valuable than anyone else's media profile or status.

If you are like me, as you search for answers, you desire Christlike mentors like Carol who can help you navigate the ups and downs of womanhood. You want to know that you matter. That you're seen, heard, and have a singular identity beyond what this world tells you to be.

That's why I'm passionate about Carol's message in *Significant*. Carol shows us how much we matter to God and to the world He has created. She takes us to the wisdom and truth of the Word of God and reveals how we can live joyfully and courageously with genuine purpose, becoming all that our Creator designed us to be.

—*Amy Groeschel*
Cofounder, Life.Church
Founder, Branch15, a nonprofit housing ministry for women

A Personal Word from Carol

Did you know that as I write my books, I picture you, the reader, across the kitchen table from me? It's true, I do. Sometimes—please don't laugh—I even set an empty mug across the table to remind myself that I am writing to another real, flesh-and-blood woman!

"Let Me Be a Woman"

Significant is the book that I have yearned to write ever since I was a young woman in college and was deeply impacted by Elisabeth Elliot's classic work *Let Me Be a Woman*. That book, which Elisabeth wrote in the form of advice to her daughter, Valerie, on the brink of her marriage, taught me, in every way that mattered, how to be a woman of value and purpose. Elisabeth knew that the only way a woman could exert any lasting influence on her culture was to embrace the truths found in the Word of God.

I remember longing to have a profound influence on a generation of women the way Elisabeth did on the young women of my own generation.

I aspired, even at the naive age of twenty-two, to be a voice of wisdom and purpose for the women who would come after me.

The years flew by, and soon I was a young mother who was homeschooling her brood of five creative, active children. Every school-day morning at ten, I sent the children off to read alone or to go outside to play so that I could turn on my little transistor radio and listen to *Gateway to Joy*, the thirty-minute program that Elisabeth Elliot hosted for many years. In that season of my life, I was smitten by her knack for calling me out of the daily routine of dishes, laundry, and little sleep to a sacred place of loving and serving the Savior. Elisabeth reminded me time after time that even the mundane can be transformed into a place of beautiful worship. Even today, I can still hear her voice saying, "Anything, if offered to God, can and will become your gateway to joy."

Isn't it interesting to realize that a person you have never met has the ability to change your life? As I have learned from so many people whom I have never met in person, I hope that my voice will not just be static in your world, but that you will clearly hear and take to heart the life-changing truths I present in this book. You can be assured that these truths have been gleaned by a real woman who has embraced the fulfillment and joy that comes from submitting her life to God's abundant calling.

I Have Been There and Done It All!

As I look back over the years of my life, which have gone by so quickly, I sometimes think that I have truly done it all! I often tell my five adult children, "When you look at me, you might think that you see a grandmother whose days are numbered. However, what you don't see is the reality that I am still…"

+ a little girl who loves to read voraciously or practice the piano rather than go outside and play.

+ a teenager who is struggling to fit in without compromising her faith.

+ an eighteen-year-old college freshman who is desperately homesick and wishes she could be little again.

+ a twenty-year-old who can't wait to write her first book.

+ a bride who is definitely head over heels in love with her groom!

+ a devastated woman whose life has been ravaged by infertility and depression.

+ a young mom whose heart has been forever changed by the wonder of holding a newborn baby in her arms.

+ a motivated woman who has been offered the position of her dreams and wonders if she should climb the corporate ladder or give herself completely to the family that she and her husband have created.

+ a home-school mother of five precocious, strong-willed children who is trying to figure out a way to make sure that they each receive enough of her time and attention.

+ an empty nester who can't believe that her kids had the nerve to grow up and leave!

+ a determined woman whose body has been invaded by cancer but who chooses to use her pain as a springboard for ministry.

And yes, I am indeed a grandmother, as well—whose favorite name is now "Marmee."

I am not sure if my life experiences have *qualified* me to write this book, but I know that I have surely been *called* to write it. I want all women to know their eternal value, to understand their God-given purpose, and to walk in their sacred calling in life. You are the woman I am writing to, my friend! As a matter of fact, if you are bold enough, don't be afraid to tell others, "Carol wrote a book just for me!"

Features of This Book

Part 1 of *Significant*, entitled "You Are…a Woman," is written in a more casual and personal style than I usually write. I am hoping that these first three chapters might draw you into developing a friendship with me. I am trusting that if I can offer the possibility of friendship, you might be captivated enough to read on. So, perhaps the first section will seem more like journal entries, blog posts, or even a sequence of friendly letters. But there is much more to come! And in the spirit of friendship, let me give you my e-mail address. You can write to me any day at carol@carolmcleodministries.com.

The other parts of the book are much like what my readers have come to expect from my writing style. We will celebrate together the cultures from which God's Word was written, we will dig deeply for treasure in the original biblical languages, and we will apply the Scriptures' unchanging principles to our lives today. We will discover together that the Bible is personal and practical as well as profound!

Another aspect of this book that I believe you will enjoy, which I've also included in other books, is that at the end of every chapter, there is a quote that pertains to the content or theme of that portion of the book. At first, I thought that I would only quote the words of women, but honestly, I decided not to be discriminatory and to allow a few men to spout their wisdom as well! The quotes are challenging, comforting, and intriguing—so, read away!

As you read *Significant*, you will notice that I often call you "my friend" or "dear friend." This is because I was thinking about you specifically at that moment. You were on my heart, and I believe on God's heart, as well, as I wrote particular words of encouragement to you. So, if you discover those terms of friendship within a phrase or sentence, just remind yourself that you are a woman who is continually on the mind and heart of God, our loving Father.

I hope that you will find yourself in the pages of this book. I pray that the Holy Spirit will revitalize your life with His power and enthusiasm. I pray that you will begin today to live the *Significant* life that God has planned for you!

Blessings, my friend.

⌣⌒

"There is not one way to be a perfect woman—but a million

ways to be a great one!"[1]

---

1. Adapted from a saying about motherhood attributed to Jill Churchill: "There's no way to be a perfect mother and a million ways to be a good one."

Introduction:
The Search for Significance

I am a woman—with all of the unique attributes, inherent strengths, and numerous foibles that are attached to a human being of my glorious gender. *I am a significant woman.* And yet, at times, I still find myself wondering who I really am.

I wonder if I will ever be "enough." I wonder if my efforts at contributing to this world are actually making a difference. I wonder if I can handle the constant and enormous stress that relentlessly engulfs me. I wonder if my feelings matter to anyone other than myself. I wonder if I am a prisoner to the mistakes of my past. I wonder….

However, as a woman of faith, I must emphatically recognize the fact that my Creator designed me with specific abilities and purposes, and that He planned these unique and recognizable attributes for me in His mind and heart in eternity past. I am certainly not perfect—but I am perfectly made by Him. I know that I am not flawless—but the One who created Me makes no mistakes.

What Does "Significance" Mean?

Women of all generations, and at every juncture in human history, have ached for purpose. Today, many women are starving for fulfillment, and they are passionately chasing significance. More than at any other time in human existence, women feel the singular call to greatness and to the possibility of making a glowing difference during their brief lifetimes.

I recently had the amazing opportunity to have lunch with a weathered Southern woman who has lived for eighty-eight years. My college roommate, Debby, often introduces me to interesting and laudable characters. Debby's mother roomed with this fascinating octogenarian when they were young women attending university.

She was so excited to spend time with me, an author, because she just loves to read—often reading three to four books per week. I, on the other hand, was thrilled to spend time with her and to just drink in from her life experiences and gathered wisdom. Yet, when I asked her what was the most significant thing that she had accomplished in her life, she responded by saying, "Oh, I have lived a rather ordinary, average life."

I was incredulous at her response! This well-educated and accomplished woman had been a professor at a well-known university for nearly forty years. As a popular physical education instructor at the university, she had taught some of the most celebrated athletes of the past half-century. She regaled me with tales of famous athletes being late for class or flunking the swimming test, and how they had eventually made millions of dollars but still sent her Christmas cards. She spoke of former students who had become university presidents, doctors, judges, and pastors. And yet, my extraordinary new friend still insisted that she had lived an average life.

I asked her about gender discrimination during her tenure at the Southern university, and she assured me that she had never experienced bias based upon the fact that she was a woman. She responded quietly but confidently that she had always been respected in the academic world and had been given the same opportunities as the men who had possessed the same level of education. Now remember, this woman had been a professor at a university in the deep South from 1960 to 1998, and yet she felt secure in her role as a woman.

I think that what troubled me, after Debby and I dropped her off at her retirement center, was that she didn't realize what a significant and vital life she had lived! While she was in awe of me, I was actually the one who was in the jaw-dropping company of an astounding woman who had no idea of her worth or her impact. And then, I soberly realized that perhaps most of us suffer from the same type of "amnesia" that my aged friend had embraced. We have forgotten that in order to live a truly significant life, we must simply leave a positive impact on those who surround us. With faithfulness and kindness, she had accomplished the call to leave a positive impact on those who walked beside her.

Purpose, Identity, Stress, and Loneliness

There are other complicated issues that hinder a woman's ability and desire to live the significant life that uniquely belongs to her. Two such issues that are common to all women—regardless of their socioeconomic level, education, marital status, or season in life—are *identity* and *purpose*. While a woman tries to figure out who she is and why she was created, all other matters in life seem to disappear. Those other concerns are dwarfed by the enormity of the questions "Who am I?" and "Why am I?"

Such weighty questions, which have always vigorously challenged women, are not mere speed bumps we occasionally encounter in life, but they often take on the massive nature of a towering mountain that overshadows our lives. Even more than that, these enormous challenges can seem like a formidable mountain range! Figuring out one's unique purpose and individual significance can be as mentally and emotionally challenging as a complicated physics equation would be to a grade-school child.

In addition to identity and purpose, two other issues common to women are *stress* and *loneliness*, each of which impacts our quest for significance. The problem of stress was recently highlighted in a *New York Times* article:

> Women are twice as likely to suffer from severe stress and anxiety as men, according to a 2016 study published in *The Journal of Brain & Behavior*. The American Psychological Association reports a gender gap year after year showing that women consistently report higher stress levels. Clearly, a stress gap exists.[2]

Women who are mothers often experience the stress of parenting, of providing financially for their families (as a contributor to the household finances or as the primary breadwinner), of juggling activities, and of keeping the home. Single women, whether they have never been married, are divorced, or are widowed, can experience the stress of making decisions alone, of others' expectations, of the demands of work, of having adequate finances, and of taking care of household repairs. Career women can experience the particular stress of dealing with high-pressure workplaces, climbing the corporate ladder, coping with challenging people in the business world, and being paid significantly less than their male counterparts. Whether she is married or single, a career woman must also maintain a stable home life while juggling the multiple plates that her profession throws her way. Every woman, whether she is married or single, whether she stays at home full-time to raise her children or pursues a vocation outside the home, also contends with the moral temptations that a confused culture offers up to her on a golden platter.

And then there is the dull ache of loneliness that hounds many women night and day.

Loneliness is not an issue that only single women must grapple with—sometimes the loneliest among us are young mothers whose days are filled with the demands of children, while they feel like no one is listening to

2. Kristin Wong, "There's a Stress Gap Between Men and Women. Here's Why It's Important," *New York Times*, November 14, 2018, https://www.nytimes.com/2018/11/14/smarter-living/stress-gap-women-men.html.

them. And even as social media has connected people, it has also cultivated isolation by encouraging its users to compare themselves negatively to others—not through actual conversations with them, but by reading their well-meaning posts, which seem to present their lives and families as "perfect."

The combination of a lack of purpose, a misguided identity, stress, and loneliness seem to throw a knock-out punch to women of this generation. When a woman finally conquers just one of these "big four," she faces the onslaught of another one coming directly her way.

I know—I have stood on a dangerous precipice where I have been cornered by all four of these enemies. I have wondered if I would even survive, and if I did survive, whether I would have the stamina to move ahead in life. Perhaps you are at such a place today.

Where Are the Answers?

It is easy for women who are looking for answers in their quest for value and purpose to begin at the wrong place—or certainly to ask the wrong questions initially. If we start with the daunting question "Who am I?" we might embark on that proverbial wild goose chase that culminates in an impossible dead end. Similarly, if we base our value and substance upon the erratic answer to the question "How do I *feel* about my worth?" we may never arrive at truth. Feelings often do not lead to either truth or peace. Our identity and purpose must be founded upon something more substantive than our emotions. Feelings are not facts.

Perhaps it is not eruptive feelings, but rather the opinions of others, from which you are extracting your value as a woman. It is certainly scriptural and ultimately hopeful to be encouraged by the counsel of other people, but it can also be undeniably devastating to be critiqued or ignored by those same people. As wonderful as their intentions may be, other people do not always lead us to truth, genuine identity, value, or significance. Your true identity is who you are regardless of your circumstances and despite of what others think of you.

If you sincerely desire to understand your significance and your eternal value, you must start by examining the motives and character of the One who created you. If you earnestly thirst for relief from stress and loneliness, you must build the foundation of your life on something that is both divine and eternal. God says powerful and glorious truths about you as a woman! So, let's start at the beginning as we explore our value as women made in His image, and then discover how to overcome issues in our lives that have seemed to negate our intrinsic worth and significance. It is time to be the woman that God created you to be!

⌒

"I am a woman above everything else."
—*Jacqueline Kennedy*

PART ONE

You Are...a Woman!

1

The Wonder of YOU!

Believe it or not, I am among the minority of Americans still alive today who spent part of their early education in a one-room schoolhouse. It's true—I commenced my days of reading, writing, and arithmetic in a century-old building that housed kindergarten through the prestigious sixth grade.

How excited I was to sit in the same places where my mother and grandfather had sat decades before my time. I mused about who had written on the blackboard prior to my school years, and who had made lifelong friendships in that single room with its timeworn desks, installed in the antiquated style of being bolted to the floor. As an intimidated five-year-old, I would gaze up at the pictures of George Washington and Abraham Lincoln that hung imposingly over the teacher's grand desk and wonder if those men were actually staring down at me!

Mrs. Dombrowski, an Australian war bride, was my teacher for three glorious years, from kindergarten through the second grade. I loved being her student! She must have seen my potential, because she challenged me from the start. She allowed me to study arithmetic with the second graders when I was only in kindergarten. She handed me books that were above my reading level, believing that I could master them. She would daily call me to her desk and whisper in my ear some amazing fact from history or science. As I would stare at her in jaw-dropping wonder, her brown eyes would twinkle at my incredulity, and then she would send me back to my desk next to the other five-year-old students.

"To Thine Own Self Be True"

The one-room schoolhouse became the victim of centralization and was closed after I finished second grade. When it came time to advance to Mrs. Cayea's third-grade class at the centralized school, I sobbed on and off for days. I couldn't imagine leaving the safety of Mrs. Dombrowski's classroom and going to school every day to listen to some other teacher whom I knew wouldn't love me nearly as much as Mrs. Dombrowski did.

This is what my beloved teacher wrote in my second-grade yearbook (I still have this treasured keepsake):

This above all: to thine own self be true,
And it must follow, as the night, the day,
Thou canst not then be false to any man.
—William Shakespeare[3]

What was the esteemed and admired Mrs. Dombrowski thinking? I was only seven years old, and I had no idea at all what those words meant at that childish time in my life.

I later wondered why she hadn't quoted something much more understandable and appropriate for a seven-year-old brain. It seems to me that Dr. Seuss, who was extremely popular at the time, might have been a more suitable voice from which to quote:

---

3. *Hamlet*, Act 1, Scene III.

Today you are you! That is truer than true!
There is no one alive who is you-er than you![4]

As I look back from the vantage point of time, I know now that both quotes mean nearly the same thing—and yet Mrs. Dombrowski elected to cite the Bard rather than the man who wrote *The Cat in the Hat* and *Green Eggs and Ham.*

Although she never had children of her own, with the words she wrote in my second-grade yearbook, the never-to-be-forgotten Margaret Dombrowski had chosen to convey these two very different and rich possibilities to me (the little girl who believed that her teacher walked on water):

First of all, she was encouraging me to stretch beyond the simple yet wonderful wisdom of Seuss. She was challenging this seven-year-old to think like a ten-year-old…or a fourteen-year-old…or even an adult.

Secondly, she was telling me, "Carol, I believe in you! You are made for more!" I didn't understand my teacher's carefully chosen Shakespearean quote in the second grade…or in the fourth grade…or in the sixth grade. But by the time I arrived in junior high school, I was beginning to understand the following about what my lifetime influencer had been endeavoring to communicate:

Figure out who you are…figure out why you are here.
Figure out what you believe and what you stand for!

Don't just be one of the crowd.
Don't compromise who you are to please others.

Stretch your brain!
Embrace bigger thoughts than you are able to think on
your own.

---

4. Dr. Seuss [Theodor Seuss Geisel] from *Happy Birthday to You!* originally published in 1959 by Random House.

Do you want to know what I truly believe today, more than five decades after Mrs. Dombrowski wrote those words in my black-and-white yearbook? I am convinced that the brilliant Australian war bride was declaring to an impressionable, wide-eyed daughter of the heart:

> Carol…any average second grader can enjoy Dr. Seuss, with all his quirks and colors and clever, imaginative words. But you were made for more than average. You were made for more than above average. You were made to be a person of virtue and character.
>
> Don't give in to the whims of the day and the fads of your culture. Defy whims and fads with well-chosen values and a commitment to noble character.

Why Are You Here?

I wonder if you had a Mrs. Dombrowski in your life. Did you have someone who believed in you completely and challenged you persistently? In case a Mrs. Dombrowski was missing in your life as you grew up and matured into an adult, allow me to speak in an Australian accent over the vast landscape of your heart:

> Why are you here?
>
> Why are you still sucking in the atmosphere of planet earth?

As you seek to love and serve God, are you here right now, at this moment, primarily to…

+ raise a significant family and teach your children to pray and trust the Lord?

+ minister to the needs of the sick or elderly?

+ teach children to paint or sing?

- run for public office?

- start your own business?

- write an inspirational book?

Please don't short-change your life with mediocrity—you were made for more! You were not created for average—you were made for extraordinary!

I dare you, as a woman of the twenty-first century, to know who you are, to determine why you are here, and then to be passionate about it!

Stand up for something noble. Let your unique voice be a resounding one of excellent values, immovable integrity, and passionate kindness. I know that I know that I know that there is not one *common* person reading these words today. Inside of you lies a seed of the greatness of God.

It is up to you—as an uncommon gift to this world—to fertilize your great seed, which may currently be lying dormant, with big dreams and both short-term and long-term goals.

It is up to you to pull up the weeds that surround your seed of greatness. Extract ordinariness and compromise. Remove selfishness and small thinking before they have a chance to grow.

Discover why you were born and go for it with every ounce of creativity and passion in your soul! You will make Mrs. Dombrowski proud when you determine not only what you were made to do but, more important, *who you were meant to be*.

Many years ago, profound words from the brilliant and well-known Shakespeare were deposited in my innocent soul by a woman of great character and intellect. Today, allow me to humbly share with you some vibrant words that have the potential to shake your very soul as you own them:

When God wants a great work done in the world or a great wrong righted, He goes about it in a very unusual way. He doesn't stir up His earthquakes or send forth His thunderbolts. Instead, He has a helpless baby born, perhaps in a simple home and of some obscure mother. And then God puts the idea into the mother's heart, and she puts it into the baby's mind. And then God waits. The greatest forces in the world are not the earthquakes and the thunderbolts. The greatest forces in the world are babies.[5]

You were born into this world some eighteen...twenty-seven...thirty-four...forty-nine...sixty-three or more years ago, as a baby into which a great idea was deposited. As a woman, you have infinitely more potential than an earthquake or a thunderbolt will ever have! God has been waiting for you to become the force you were made to be!

$$\sim$$

"The issue is not if you are going to die, because none of us gets out of here alive! The issue is: did you live the life you were created to on earth?"
—*Author unknown*

---

5. E. T. Sullivan [Reverend Edward Taylor Sullivan] in *The Treasure Chest*, ed. Charles L. Wallis (New York: Harper and Row, 1965), 53.

2

It's Time

In a unique and powerful way, women are often the leading members of God's search and rescue team. When God's heart is pursuing a lost person, He frequently sends a woman on the chase. Women have been especially created to extravagantly nurture and lavishly protect people who need a bit of practical help and some tender loving care.

God should know what women are capable of—He created us just the way we are for His particular purposes! May I just interject here that God's purpose for your life should be your purpose for your life? There should be no self-justifications or excuses for going our own way. Instead, the cry of our hearts must daily be, "My life for God's will!" Yet we often misunderstand or underestimate what His will for us is.

For much of my life, I was content to be a "nurse" who quietly, gently, and kindly gave encouragement to those who were bruised and shattered on the battlefield of life. What joy and delight I have experienced in fulfilling that role of mercy! I have loved being a vital part of God's "Red

Cross"—encouraging my husband, nurturing children, and praying with broken women, offering them hope. I have deeply enjoyed caring for my mother and mother-in-law as they age, and quietly serving others whom God has brought into my wonderful life. And I will continue to do those things as long as there is breath in my soul. Women were created by the Giver of all life to bring life into our world. This divine calling—that of giving life—can be accomplished through various expressions, acts of service, and creative genius.

Yet I do believe that life is seasonal for women, and we have to be prepared to change our hats and take on new job descriptions willingly and quickly. How sad to believe that you can only be what you were twenty years ago! How wonderful to know that you are worthy of change and even advancement in the kingdom of God!

In this book, I intend to stretch you and help you to dream dreams that you may never have thought possible. I am determined to convince you that regardless of your education, income, station in life, weight, marital status, or age, you are a significant woman and your Creator has plans to use you in an unparalleled manner.

A New Season of Purpose

In the Scriptures, we see that God used women for specific purposes and assignments. His methods have not changed, because He is a God who is consistent in His plans: *"For I, the LORD, do not change"* (Malachi 3:6).

God entrusted Eve to be the mother of all the living, despite the troubling fact that Eve had doubted Him and then given in to sin.

God chose Sarah to give birth to a baby boy whose descendants would become a great nation, even though, at age ninety, her cheeks were wrinkled and her body was about as ripe as a dried-up prune!

God elected Esther, a victim of sexual trafficking, to save a people.

God picked the obscure Deborah to serve as a judge over a nation.

God used a homemaker named Hannah and her desperate prayers to change the course of a nation's history.

God appointed Rahab, a prostitute, to help the people of God win a great victory.

God chose a young, grieving widow named Ruth to be part of the line of the Messiah as she quietly believed in His intervention when all natural hope was gone.

God selected Elizabeth, a righteous, older woman, to raise a strong-willed boy who would prepare the way of the Lord.

God appointed Mary, a teenage virgin, to give birth to the Savior of the world.

God chose Mary Magdalene to demonstrate that a woman who had formerly been trapped in the demonic darkness of sin could have the propensity to lavishly love her Savior and minister to Him when others chose to judge and ridicule Him.

Have you seen yourself in this cast list yet? Do you feel that God just might be calling you out of your insecurities so you can move past your place of pain or stagnation and into a new season of purpose? Would you accept a change in assignment or in possibility?

Dreaming with the Father

Consider this additional question: Would you take some time today to dream with the Father and to hear His voice concerning the years that you have remaining on earth—whether it is one year or fifty years?

As I was dreaming with God recently, He spoke a word to my heart that has emphatically changed my focus and my job description: "Carol, you are in the army now!"

If you knew me, you would understand how absurd that is in the natural course of who I am and how I have been wired as a woman. I am a woman who loves peace, who quietly encourages others, and who desperately needs creature comforts. And yet, I heard the voice of my Father say, "It is time for women to go to war!"

There is a battle raging for the lives of men, women, and children, and it is time for the women of this generation to exert their influence and their power to strategically battle on behalf of those who are caught in the crossfire. It is time for us to believe that we are significant and to respond as such.

We must discern what our specific role and calling in life is. Perhaps you have been called to care for the wounded, which is a powerful and significant assignment! Serve well as you meet the needs of the broken with compassion and kindness. But perhaps, like me, you are called to join the army of God at this exciting moment in history. We are the ones who must rise up and fight so that there will no longer be so many who need critical care. We must lend our voices, our hearts, our gifts, and our time to the Great Commission and to the battle to prevent others from experiencing pain.

It's time for today's women of God to rise up against the powers of darkness, against the slavery of sexual predators, against the thief of depression, and against the lie of eating disorders.

It's time for the women of God of this generation to say, "No more!" to abuse, to pornography, to addictions, and to self-harm.

It's time for the women of God to raise a standard of moral purity, to demonstrate the strength that is extracted only from the joy of His presence, and to live the abundant life that Jesus alone can give.

It's time.

I believe that God is raising up a generation of "Esthers." He is not raising up just one Esther, but He is raising up an entire generation of women who have been born *"for such a time as this"* (Esther 4:14). God is raising up a generation of women who know the power of fasting, who are not intimidated by the compromise of the culture, and who are willing to stand against demonic spirits. God is raising up a generation of women who are not afraid of dying, but who are determined to live boldly and courageously on the battlefield of life.

What will your role be? Because you will, indeed, play a role in the plan of God during your lifespan. Will you cower or will you care? Will you be afraid or will you be a force to be reckoned with? Will you truly live or will you merely die?

It's time for the women of God to go to "war." It's time.

⌒

"Holy Spirit, think through me till
Your ideas are my ideas."
—*Amy Carmichael*

3

A Few Good Women

May I just leave one more piece of encouragement to guide you on your way before we dig deeply in the Word of God in the chapters to follow? I hope that this quote, spoken over a century ago by General William Booth, the founder of the Salvation Army, will send a chill up your spine and give you reason to set your gaze defiantly to the future: "Some of my best men are women!"

Isn't *that* an interesting quote from one of the most powerful Christian leaders of the nineteenth century? With his high estimation of the female gender and its capabilities, he certainly was a man before his time. It was nearly a century later, in 1975, that *Time* magazine gave its "Man of the Year" award to "American women."

"Some of my best men are women!" Now that you've considered these profound words for a moment, let me stretch you just a bit farther....

I wonder if the same words are not also in the heart and mind of God at our moment in history. I wonder if, when the Father looks down from

His bird's-eye view of all that is happening on the earth today, He turns to His Son, seated at His right side, and, with a twinkle in His eye, echoes the words of William Booth: "Some of My best men are women!" And I wonder if the Holy Spirit, who is most certainly eavesdropping on the conversation, raises His fist in the air in complete agreement with the Father.

God is looking for "a few good men" and "a few good women" to make a difference in His kingdom at every juncture in history. Perhaps the Father, who created all of us in His heart of love, is not as concerned with the gender on our birth certificate as He is with the condition of our heart.

I will pour out My Spirit on all mankind; and your sons and daughters will prophesy.... Even on the male and female servants I will pour out My Spirit in those days.   —Joel 2:28–29

Now, more than ever, women need to understand their important role and their significance in the call and intent of God. God's plan is that His Holy Spirit endue humanity, both male and female, with power from on high. Men and women receive the same power in the same measure. The power that both men and women receive from the Holy Spirit includes the ability to be courageous witnesses and to fulfill the God-given mandate that is particular to each generation.

What is God calling you to do through the power of His Holy Spirit? The days of cowering in fear, hiding behind insignificance, and wallowing in lack of opportunities are over. God is blowing doors wide open for women as never before. It is time for us to march forward in grand anticipation of all that God can do through even one woman who is submitted to the call of God and filled with His Spirit.

A woman's voice in the marketplace, in the church, and in the home offers a perspective and a tone that is valuable and unique. We are not fragile clones of our male counterparts; rather, we have been outstandingly fashioned by the God of the universe for a role in the story of humanity that is utterly feminine, powerfully impactful, and undoubtedly irreplaceable.

The Holy Spirit of Pentecost has been poured out upon your life! What will you do with this gift? Don't waste these days of power and open doors! When Peter received the Holy Spirit, thousands of people were saved. When John received the Holy Spirit, lame men walked. When Paul received the Holy Spirit, prison walls fell down.

I believe that God is looking at your life, this very day, and, with a twinkle in His eye, He is reminding you that some of His very best men, indeed, are women! *Significant women.*

⌁

"We are women, and my plea is, Let me be a woman,
holy through and through, asking for nothing but what God
wants to give me, receiving with both hands and
with all my heart whatever that is."
—*Elisabeth Elliot*

PART TWO

You Are...a Woman of
Unmatched Purpose

4

On Purpose...for Purpose... with Purpose

Yo were made on purpose, for purpose, and with purpose! What an extraordinary—but sadly, often disbelieved—truth! May I make that statement again so that you can allow the power of the words to sink deeply into your purpose-parched soul?

You were made on purpose...for purpose...and with purpose!

You must not allow any person or situation to convince you of anything to the contrary.

Your circumstances may endeavor to persuade you that you will never walk in your life's destiny. Don't believe them.

Your culture may attempt to strip you of your God-ordained purpose. You must defiantly believe His Word and lay bare the lies of the culture.

Your feelings will undoubtedly shout at you, endeavor to manipulate you, and then cause you to minimize the purpose that is eternally yours. Remind yourself daily that your feelings are not the author of all truth. God is.

Even well-meaning people may try to convince you that your purpose is less than what you were created to fulfill. You must learn whose advice to listen to attentively and whose to resolutely ignore at every juncture in life.

Allow me to affirm this truth one more time: *you were made on purpose, for purpose, and with purpose.* Your life matters to the plans of God at your moment in history. You are the only person just like you whom God has ever created in all of eternity past or will create in all of eternity future. There has never been anyone like you in all of recorded history. There is no one else like you today, and there will never be anyone like you in all of the ages to come. No one else has exactly your genetic makeup, your fingerprints, or the number of hairs on your head. How astounding!

The First Time in Forever

I'll never forget seeing the movie *The Sound of Music* with my family when I was in the third grade. It was the first movie my parents took me to see, other than *The Greatest Story Ever Told*. (We were a dedicated Christian family of the 1960s, and movies were not high on our priority list!) I was captivated by this film, from the first twirl that Maria took upon a mountaintop in Austria to the final song that played as the family Von Trapp trekked over the same mountain range into freedom in Switzerland. My eight-year-old heart thumped out of my chest as I watched Maria wriggle her way into the lives and hearts of seven rambunctious and undisciplined but extremely musical children.

My love affair with musicals, which began passionately during the early years of my life, has not abated to this day! I can sing the songs of musicals in my sleep and have taught the lyrics of tune after tune to my grandchildren. There is just something about the melodies from a grand musical that have the ability to put a spring in your step and a sparkle in your eyes!

My sweet granddaughter Olivia knows how much I love musicals, and several years ago, while I was visiting her family in Texas, she wanted to have a "Girls' Movie Night" with me. Being the accommodating Marmee that I am, I simply couldn't resist her request. On her "watch list" for the night was a new musical that had recently become available on DVD. She could hardly wait to commence our evening together—which included manicures, complete with fingernail polish, and the grand event of eating popcorn and viewing *Frozen* with her doting grandmother!

As we watched the creative tale unfold, I tried to focus on the setting, the main characters, and the scenery. But it was truly the company that I enjoyed to the fullest degree. However, my heart stopped in its middle-aged beating when the melody and lyrics of "For the First Time in Forever" interrupted the otherwise predictable fairy tale.

Once the movie was over and Olivia had fallen into the sweet sleep of childhood on my bed, I watched that particular scene time after time after time. I listened to the song with tears falling down my cheeks, and I quickly committed the lyrics to memory. Yet it wasn't the lyrics that touched me in such a deep and passionate manner—it was the voice of the eternal Holy Spirit, who sang a duet with this song from the early twenty-first century. The Holy Spirit whispered to my discouraged heart, "Carol, you are God's first-time-in-forever!"

My sister and my friend, you, too, are God's "first-time-in-forever creation"—and you are vital to His purposes! Remember, you must not allow your culture, your circumstances, your emotions, or other people to convince you otherwise. History would be incomplete without your biography. If history were to subtract the imprint of your heart, all of creation would walk away in disappointment. And God's eternal "forever" would be incomplete without your personality and gifts, because their absence would leave a great vacuum that would be impossible to fill with anyone else's personality and gifts.

I hope that knowing you are God's first-time-in-forever creation is comforting and even compelling to you, but we have yet to address the questions that are likely nipping at the heels of your soul: "Why am I here?" "What is my story meant to be?" "What is my exact purpose in life?"

Your Purpose in One Sentence

It only takes one sentence to explain definitively why your existence on planet earth in the first part of the twenty-first century is so important to the plans of God and to eternity. It is not necessary for you to consult the insights of philosophers or the theories of psychologists in order to comprehend your purpose. You can understand your overall assignment with this simple but profound truth:

You are here to reveal the story of Jesus!

Dear friend, you are here so that Jesus can be present in the flesh through you.

If you don't reveal Jesus to other people through the power of His Spirit, who will?

If you don't tell the story of Jesus with your life, who will?

If you don't love difficult people as He has loved you, who will do the difficult loving?

If you are not good, as He is always good, who will be good?

If you are not kind, as He is unspeakably kind, who will be kind?

Your life, dear friend, will only be as significant as your choice to lay down your life and tell the story of Jesus. The overriding, driving purpose of your life is to reveal Jesus to others!

I can assure you that you won't be distracted by comparing yourself to other people if you are captivated by your purpose. No one can reveal the story of Jesus like you can! You are God's first-time-in-forever.

Valuable and Esteemed

You saw me before I was born. Every day of my life was recorded in your book. Every moment was laid out before a single moment had passed. How precious are your thoughts about me, O God. They cannot be numbered! I can't even count them; they outnumber the grains of sand! And when I wake up, you are still with me!

—Psalm 139:16–18 (NLT)

If you believe the truths of Scripture, then you must believe that before you were even born, the God of the universe had you on His mind. You are not here by accident or by mistake; you are here by the intentional purposes and plans of God. In the above verse, the psalmist David proclaimed, *"How precious are your thoughts about me, O God."* Think about that for a moment! An ordinary man, who was often entrapped in discouragement and depression, exclaimed from the depths of his being that his Creator— the One who had fashioned him—thought wonderful thoughts about His creation!

Let's linger on the word *"thoughts,"* which is the Hebrew word *rea'*, because its meaning in the original language has rich texture and marvelous variance of definition. That word refers to what God thinks about you, but it can also embrace the idea of *purpose* or *aim*. Allow that powerful detail to sink into your heart as you ponder the direction of your life this side of heaven.

Not only does God, your heavenly Father, have a purpose for your life, but the psalmist describes what type of purpose is in His wonderful mind. His purpose for your life is *"precious"*! The Hebrew word that describes the thoughts and plans of God toward your significant life is *yaqar*. This word does, indeed, mean "to be precious," but it can also be translated as "to be esteemed, valued, treasured, and costly." It encompasses the idea of being prized and extremely valuable. The purpose that God has attached to your life is valuable to Him and to His kingdom.

You are a woman of worth and value.

Basing your identity and the value of your purpose on the blueprint of the One who made you is essential to determining a true estimation of yourself. Your Creator thinks cherished thoughts about your life! The One who fashioned your innermost parts has priceless plans and esteemed goals in store for you.

God thought about you before you were even a twinkle in your earthly father's eye. Before you were rocked in your mother's arms, before you slept through the night, before you learned how to take your first, wobbling baby steps, He was thinking about you and planning for your grand entrance onto the stage of history. Your heavenly Father spent eternity past planning who you would be and how He would use you today in this world. Your life was not accidental but intentional; it was carefully thought out and conceived in His eternal heart and immeasurable mind.

God meant for the minutes of your life to matter greatly during your brief tenure on planet earth. Doesn't that bring joy to your heart? He thought about you and prepared for you! You are His first-time-in-forever creation!

⌒

"My deepest awareness of myself is that I am deeply loved by Jesus Christ and I have done nothing to earn it or deserve it."
—*Brennan Manning,* The Ragamuffin Gospel

5

Plans? What Plans?

Do you have a favorite quote that has steered the course of your life? Perhaps you "own" a lyric from a well-loved song that seems to reach deeply into the corners of your heart. A familiar and well-loved Scripture passage that I learned in my childhood has been a constant source of direction and comfort to me over the years. Maybe you know these ancient yet still-potent verses, or have at least heard the first sentence quoted:

> *"For I know the plans that I have for you," declares the* LORD, *"plans for welfare and not for calamity to give you a future and a hope. Then you will call upon Me and come and pray to Me, and I will listen to you. You will seek Me and find Me when you search for Me with all your heart. I will be found by you," declares the* LORD, *"and I will restore your fortunes and will gather you from all the nations...."*
> —Jeremiah 29:11–14

5

Every time I read this passage, it seems as if a blanket of supernatural peace and blessed assurance is gently wrapped around the relentless, cold questions and the nagging, fractious issues of my soul. There is intrinsic power in knowing that the God of the universe not only created me but also has a plan for me. He didn't create me and then leave me to desperately try to discover some significance for my existence. He didn't expect me to find my own way along this rugged pathway called life. He didn't presuppose that in my own strength, I would be able to navigate my pain. Instead, He wisely and brilliantly mapped out the plan for my life first—and then He created me. First came God's conceptualization of me in His great purposes, and then came the actualization of me in His grand creation.

Your life, like mine, is not random. Our Creator has definite plans for every single one of our days—and He shares them with us in His Word and by His Spirit.

My Favorite Words in Scripture

When I study the thoughts and ideas contained in the Bible, I ravenously search for meaning and substance behind each word and phrase. I often say, "Oh, this is my favorite verse!" or, "Oh, this is my favorite Hebrew word!"—and I can hear my friends tittering behind my back. As they sweetly roll their eyes and shake their heads in my direction, they all know that *everything* in the Bible is my favorite. But how I love to point out those words and phrases that are especially compelling to me in my current study of God's Word!

May I share with you one of my absolute favorite words in Scripture? (It's okay with me if you grin at the knowledge that this is one of my "thousands" of favorite words in the sacred pages.) It is the word *"plans"* found in Jeremiah 29:11. Written by an opinionated, extroverted prophet by the name of Jeremiah, this word is one of the most potent Hebrew terms in all of Scripture. Are you ready to be gobsmacked?

The word translated *"plans"* is *machashabah*; however, *machashabah* means so much more than mere "plans." This ancient, multilayered word can also be translated as "thought," "device," "intention," "purpose," "invention," "imagination," or "artistic work." If you go searching for buried treasure in *machashabah*, you will be certain to find it there!

Jeremiah, by the unction of the Spirit, deeply desired that God's people would thoroughly understand what His unconditional posture toward their lives is—and what it always will be for eternity. That is why I can tell you this: You are a work of art. Even more than that, my friend, you are God's masterpiece! You are His magnum opus, and you will never be able to talk Him out of His high opinion concerning who He created you to be!

The Reason "Why"

God's preplanning for your unmatched life was thorough, complete, and purposeful. He contemplated who you would become and how He would be able to use you, making a list of all of the people who would be impacted by your influence. We often ponder the "why" of our lives. If you have a natural bent toward science, there is a divine reason "why." If you are a gifted musician, there is a sacred and eternal reason "why." If you love words and spend your free hours digesting books, there is a supernatural reason "why." If you are an excellent administrator and have a knack for organization, there is an unmistakable reason "why." If you love hanging out with children and have the sweet patience that it requires to listen to their words and to engage in their activities, there is a powerful reason "why."

You are who you are by divine plan and eternal calling. You must never dismiss your gifts, talents, interests, and deepest desires as unimportant or disposable. You were created under divine authority and supervision, and every cell in your body was crafted with care, love, and attention to the minutest of details.

Your "why" is most decidedly different from my "why"—and it is that way by design. The wonder of it all is that your "why" and my "why"—although extremely different—are both able to reflect the unmistakable glory of God. Always remember that the Creator God designed only one of you in all of eternity past and in all of eternity yet to come. Your creation was magnificent and meaningful. Quite simply, you matter!

You matter to God...you matter to the world in which you live...you matter to history...and you matter to eternity. Your "why" is perpetually knocking at the door of your heart in order to be realized. God designed your "why," and now you get to gloriously spend your life living it out!

Made for NOW!

There are many people in our culture who believe that there is a God, but that He has merely thrown each of us into the universe as a random clump of cells. This belief, which depicts an arbitrary action of God, is followed up by the philosophy that God glibly assumes these random cells will find their own reason for existence and their own way in life. My friend, nothing could be further from the truth!

When God made you, He chose the time period and the geographical location(s) in which you would live. However, His preplanning for your life held even more specificity than when and where you would exist: you are here, at this moment in human history, to discover God and all that He is:

And He made from one man every nation of mankind to live on all the face of the earth, having determined their appointed times and the boundaries of their habitation, that they would seek God, if perhaps they might grope for Him and find Him, though He is not far from each one of us; for in Him we live and move and exist. —Acts 17:26–28

Oh, don't you just love this extraordinary passage? Doesn't it send shivers up and down your spine? Doesn't it cause you to take a deep breath and then look up toward heaven in reverent wonder?

"Where Would You Be?"

Don't ever doubt that God made you for purpose! His intention for your life is imbedded deeply within your genetics, as well as within every molecule of your body.

God put forethought into your purpose, and then, based upon His plans for you, He determined the appointed time period of your existence. He left absolutely nothing to chance when it came to your extraordinary life! You were not designed to live during the time of the Reformation, the Industrial Revolution, or World War I. *Now* is the time for which you were created to live your significant and resplendent existence. God is strategic in all that He does, and His divine strategy was to utilize you and all that you would become in the twenty-first century. Your appointed time to serve God is *today*!

When my children were young and still living at home, we would often play a game around the dinner table entitled "Where Would You Be?" I would ask each family member which event in history they would have liked to have been present for. Sometimes, I would give them the framework of a past major sporting event or a happening from American history, but oftentimes, in order to stimulate lively conversation, I would ask them to choose which biblical event they would like to imagine themselves attending.

The boys always wanted to be at some battle or another scenario where blood and guts were part of the setting. My little males, whose testosterone was ever increasing, wanted to observe the walls of Jericho collapse, the mighty Goliath drop down dead, or those three brave young Israelites being thrown into the fiery furnace and then walking around in the flames unharmed.

My little girls, however, had different biblical preferences. They always wanted to be at the very first Christmas and hold the baby Jesus. They wanted to hear the cattle lowing, see the shepherds bowing, and listen to the angels singing.

Craig, my pastor husband, definitely wanted to be at the empty tomb with Peter and John! His face would light up with excitement as he imagined what it would have been like to hear the angel say, *"He is not here, for He has risen"* (Matthew 28:6).

And then, when it was my turn to share the one biblical event that I would have loved to have seen with my very own eyes, I, too, would always give the same answer. Time after time, meal after meal, I expressed my heart's desire to have been at the creation of the earth, when mankind walked onto the stage of history for the very first time. Can you imagine what that moment must have been like? Can you envision the gasp of heaven when God blew His own breath into the dust of the earth and man became a living being? The moment when God created Adam and Eve in His very own image was no inconsequential event. It has left ripples on the seas of eternity that have not stopped to this very day.

My friend, let me quickly remind you that when you walked onto the stage of history, you were no inconsequential event either! God created you with the same tender care and eternal value with which He created Adam and Eve. You were designed in the heart of God for such a time as this!

Groping in the Dark for God

Hidden in the beautiful pathways of that passage from Acts 17 is the reason you were born for *today*. Don't let this purposeful and fascinating truth escape you as you discover your destiny as a woman with the fingerprint of God upon her very soul. Let's read the passage again:

And He made from one man every nation of mankind to live on all the face of the earth, having determined their appointed times and the boundaries of their habitation, that they would seek God, if perhaps they might grope for Him and find Him, though He is not far from each one of us; for in Him we live and move and exist. —Acts 17:26–28

The word *"grope"* used in the above passage means "to handle, to touch, or to feel." It also encompasses the meaning of seeking for something. You were created to seek God and to inspire others to seek Him because of what they observe in your uncommon life. Your days matter to eternity, so you must be very, very careful what you choose to search for this side of heaven's glory. You live and move and have your very existence in God and in all that He is! You were made in Him and for Him. The life that is in you has been placed there because of Him. A rich part of your assignment this side of heaven is to "grope" for or to touch and feel the Lord and His kingdom in all of your choices.

Think about what it means that God strategically decided to plant your life on earth at this moment in history so that you would seek Him with every breath and fiber of your being. This is a grand and consuming purpose that should never be ignored or discounted. You are here to discover who God is, in all of His unfathomable goodness. And, you are here to share that discovery with those with whom you share the stage of history. There is no grander or more significant reason to live than that!

What Do Others See?

When others observe your life, what do they see? Do they see a woman who lives mainly to make money, is striving to earn yet another advanced degree to prove herself as admirable, or is trying to keep up with the neighbors in status and possessions? Does your circle of influence see a woman who is impatient with her husband and barely speaks to her parents? Do your friends watch as you continually weep over the empty nest, longing for the happiness of yesterday? Are your acquaintances subjected to a never-ending soliloquy about your life—your newest diet, your latest trip, or your most recent purchase?

As a woman who knows that she has been uniquely fashioned by her Creator for this exact moment in history, I remind myself daily that the things I am seeking and reaching for are being noted by other people who constantly observe my life's journey. The most wonderful and memorable part of anyone's life is their relationship with their Creator and Savior. As others observe your love for Him and your attention to Him, they, too, will be stimulated to acknowledge His presence and perhaps even honor His lordship. The most dynamic compliment that can ever be given about your life is this one: "I know Jesus better because I knew her."

Others will, indeed, seek God as they see you seeking Him.

⌒

"The two most important days in your life are the day you are
born and the day you find out why."
—*Mark Twain*

6

One Thousand Years Later

Several years ago, I was in a battle for my very life. I had been diagnosed with aggressive breast cancer and underwent five surgeries. During one of them, I nearly died. I took vile drugs and spent hours upon hours in doctors' offices and in testing facilities. As you can imagine, during that twenty-four-month period of my life, I was desperate for God! I searched the Scriptures as a dying man in the desert searches for even one drop of water. I combed through the Bible as a starving woman craves just one morsel of sustenance. I simply couldn't get enough of Him and all that He is!

As the war with cancer raged on, I would search the Scriptures for even a single taste of God's sweetness. Every morning, I sat with my Bible open on my lap, reading God's Word; every afternoon, I spent further time in Scriptures; and every evening, I ignored the television so that I could read more words on the sacred pages. God met me in my place of desperation, and I discovered treasures that sustained my soul during those dark days of treatment.

One particular verse from the book of Acts touched me deeply, and it has revolutionized my life in the days since this battle for my health. The Holy Spirit presented this Scripture to me one morning when I was up before the sun:

For David, after he had served the purpose of God in his own generation, fell asleep, and was laid among his fathers and underwent decay. —Acts 13:36

Don't Miss This!

The book of Acts, as you might know, is the account of the early church and was likely written by Luke the physician shortly after the year AD 60. King David, to whom this verse is referring, was the writer of most of the Psalms. After defeating the giant Goliath and leading the Israelites to victory over the Philistines when he was just a toothpick of a boy, he became one of the most important figures in Jewish history. Historians record that David lived from about 907 BC to 837 BC, which was just under a millennia before the book of Acts was written.

It takes my breath away when I realize that the Holy Spirit was still talking about the life of King David nearly one thousand years after he lived! Can you imagine your life possessing that type of enduring impact? I want the Holy Spirit to recount the passion of my life for Christ one thousand years after I step into eternity! Wouldn't it be amazing if, a thousand years from today, the Holy Spirit paused for a moment and then began speaking to a woman of the thirty-first century, saying, "You know, that Carol McLeod…she served the purpose of God in her own generation. She refused to die until she accomplished everything that He had preplanned for her to accomplish with her life."

God has a purpose for you in your own generation. However, you won't discover it unless you spend your entire life reaching for God and pointing others to find Him just as you have.

Purposed for Purpose

The word *purpose* has become a commonly used term in our current culture, yet it is still compelling. A number of books, including best sellers, have the word *purpose* in their title (the word is also in the subtitle of this book!). Podcasts and blogs are driven by this term, and conferences have been designed to help people explore their life callings. However, we have seen that "purpose" is not a contemporary concept; it has been in the heart of God since the beginning of time.

According to Dr. Luke and the Holy Spirit, David *"served the purpose of God in his own generation."* The Greek word for *"purpose"* in Acts 13:36 is *boule'*, which is a strong and multifaceted term. As many ancient words do, *boule'* encompasses several different meanings, which include the following: "reflection," "counsel," "will," "thoughts," "advice," and "intention." *Boule'* denotes prior deliberation concerning an intended purpose, not something spur-of-the-moment. It's a word that is meant to convey deliberation and consideration.

But what do the word *boule'*, Dr. Luke, and David have to do with your life of purpose in the twenty-first century? Read on, my friend, read on.

Since God, the Creator of the universe and the Father of all eternity, thought about your life and preplanned for your existence, He knows *that* you are here, and He knows *why* you are here. When we read that David served the purpose of God in his generation, it confirms what we noted earlier in Acts 17:26 about God's creation of all people: *"...having determined their appointed times."* So, not only did God's plan for your life require His personal reflection and counsel, but He conceived it to happen at the "appointed time." The time period in which you live has been specifically and individually determined by an all-wise and all-loving God.

Just Imagine!

For just a moment, let's play our own "time machine" game, imagining the various historical periods for which you might have been destined and intended to in live by your Creator God. You might have been born during the Dark Ages, the fatal days of the black plague, or the time when the

Pilgrims were traveling across the ocean in flimsy, wooden vessels, tossed to and fro by the waves of the icy Atlantic. Or, your time of human destiny might have been during the devastation of the Civil War, when brother was fighting against brother.

This is what I resolutely believe concerning the nature of my own life and purpose:

- If I had been chosen by God to live before the Reformation, I would have discovered my calling and found my fulfillment by being one of the scribes copying the Scriptures onto parchment for the common man to read.

- If I had lived during the 1800s, I would have joined a wagon train to take the gospel to those who lived west of the Mississippi.

- If I had lived during the first part of the twentieth century, I would have been a missionary, traveling to other lands to tell people about Jesus.

Each of these imaginary scenarios is a reflection of the gifts and calling that are uniquely mine, using the means employed by people of that particular era. But the wonder of it all is that, when the Father thought about my life and considered all that I would become, He determined that my life would extend from the second half of the twentieth century into the twenty-first century. And, as I serve His purposes unique to my own generation, I will use every method of communication available to tell the story of Jesus! I will boldly share His truth by partnering with the publishing industry. I will utilize radio, TV, blogs, podcasts, and the Internet. I will be a relentless carrier of joy on all forms of social media. And, like David, I will absolutely refuse to die until I complete the purposes of God for my life!

God intends that you and I bring something on purpose to the generation in which we live. Remind yourself daily that the Creator of the universe has thought about your life and has planned for you to live now. You can embrace a significant part of the joy this side of heaven that He longs for you to experience when you determine to live in His place of purpose.

Remind yourself often that God knows you are here and is not surprised by your existence. He has designed a well-thought-out plan that fits only the "you" that you gloriously are!

⌒

"If human beings are perceived as potentials rather than problems, as possessing strengths instead of weaknesses, as unlimited rather than dull and unresponsive, then they thrive and grow to their capabilities."
—*Barbara Bush*

7

"I Knew You"

If you are struggling with knowing or fulfilling your destiny in life, you are not alone in this particular conundrum of the soul. You are in good company with men and women who, for thousands of years before you, have paddled in the sea of purposelessness. There was one such man who was floundering for direction when God spoke a profound word to him. His name was Jeremiah.

> *Now the word of the LORD came to me saying, "Before I formed you in the womb I knew you, and before you were born I consecrated you; I have appointed you a prophet to the nations."*
>
> *—Jeremiah 1:4–5*

Wouldn't you absolutely love to have the same experience that Jeremiah had at the crossroads of uncertainty and purpose? Don't you wish that God would speak audibly and clearly in the midst of the tug-of-war that perpetually takes place between determination and confusion in the depths of your soul? Let's eavesdrop on the conversation that God had with Jeremiah to see if we might apply it to our lives as well.

When the Lord spoke to Jeremiah, He reminded him that He had known him before he was even born. This confirms what we have recognized as truth concerning God's foresight about our own lives before our grand entrance upon planet earth. We were known by the Creator of the universe, by the infinite One, before we were embryos in our mothers' wombs. He knew our strengths and our weaknesses, our talents and our preferences, our interests and our aversions before we physically existed.

Would you imagine for a moment that God has spoken the same words to you that He spoke to Jeremiah to address your confusion and angst? Would you allow the words that the Lord spoke to Jeremiah to comfort you as you grapple for meaning in your life?

You serve a God who is still speaking dreams and destiny to His beloved children, who continues to speak one-on-one with them, and it is vital that you take the time to listen to what He is saying to you personally. I actually believe that God desires to speak to you more than you desire to take the time to listen to what He has to say. Your voice is not the voice that matters in the struggle for goals and ambitions—it is His voice that casts the deciding vote. In the midst of the inner civil war for meaning in life that has wounded you time and time again, be very careful to listen for His voice.

The same God who spoke to Jeremiah is still speaking to His children today. I believe that God desires to speak to your life with the same clarity with which He spoke to Jeremiah. The Lord has scheduled your life into the history of the world and has designed you for His specific assignment. As a child of God, you don't "decide" your assignment—you discover it! As you listen for the voice of God and lean into His love for you, you will discern the sacred reason for which you were created. And what a marvelous discovery that will be!

Not Without Him

One of the aspects of discovering our assignment in life that can be puzzling at first is that it will not only showcase our talents and strengths, but it will also put on display our insecurities, weaknesses, and shortcomings. God doesn't want you to fulfill your assignment in life without His strength, power, and wisdom, which is the precise reason why your calling might cause you to tremble rather than to boast. So, if you feel God is calling you to be a doctor or nurse, don't shy away from the field of medicine just because you currently have an aversion to blood. Or, don't ignore a possible career in politics just because you usually break out in hives at the thought of public speaking. The Father loves to show off in the areas that we are lacking and to be recognized as strong in all of our weaknesses! Your calling, although specific to you, will never be accomplished without Him.

The same God who knew David and Jeremiah in their mothers' wombs knew you in your mother's womb and will enable you to fulfill what He has called you to do. Have you fully embraced the truth that He had a divine plan for you before you were even jabbering away in baby babble? That your loving Father had a strategic destiny mapped out for your life before you took your first wobbling step as a toddler? That God placed wisdom and creativity in your mind and heart before you ever learned to read the simple books of childhood?

Who, Me? Argue with God?

Admit it...you have argued with God from time to time! At certain moments of important decision or opportunity, we have all been guilty of arguing against His purposes in our vain and mortal immaturity. I am fairly certain that after the crisis passed, we were not proud of our words, our bold defiance, or the guile that was in our hearts toward a Father who deeply loves us.

Jeremiah, too, had the audacity to argue with God. He possessed a stubborn will and a heart that was confused about his calling and purpose. After God had declared to him exactly who he was and what he had been called to accomplish, Jeremiah defiantly, yet woefully, began an unnecessary dispute with his Lord.

Then I said, "Alas, Lord GOD! Behold, I do not know how to speak, because I am a youth." —Jeremiah 1:6

First of all, let me briefly coach you about etiquette before the King of all kings and the Lord of all lords: never begin a sentence with *"Alas"*! Can you just picture this scenario? Can you imagine Jeremiah throwing the back of his hand against his forehead and telling God all that he *wasn't?* The insecure young man explained to his Creator everything that he was unable to do and everything that would be impossible for him to accomplish.

Do Jeremiah's words sound familiar to you? Perhaps you have recited such a soliloquy to the Lord as you have endeavored to defend your insecurities and your lack of belief in His promises. Let me just tell you that if you feel you must begin a sentence with the four-letter word *alas*, you probably shouldn't be saying it at all!

Jeremiah told the Lord that he was too young for his assignment and that he wasn't a gifted speaker. If you have disputed with God concerning your identity and destiny, what was the gist of your argument? Perhaps you told Him that you have made too many mistakes in life or are too deeply in debt for Him to use you. Perhaps you tried to convince the Lord that you are too old, too overweight, or too exhausted. Maybe you reminded God that you had sex before marriage, have been divorced, or have had an abortion.

Excuses didn't work for Jeremiah, and they won't work for you either. Human excuses are no match for the plan of God. What you have been in the past will never stop His promises for you now or in the future. When you woefully react to the call of God by saying, "Alas, Lord! It can't be me. There is no way that You can use my life," He responds with a knowing grin on His face. He reminds His obstinate and argumentative child, "Oh, yes, it can be you! It can be you because you have Me!"

It's Not Fair to Compare

One of my biggest weaknesses in life is that I tend to compare myself with other women. Don't you? I compare my small and modestly furnished brick home with their extremely large and fabulously decorated dream homes. I have been known to compare the behavior of my children with the behavior of the perfectly mannered, overachieving young adults who belong to other moms. I compare my wardrobe, my weight, my writing, the success of my ministry, and the size of my bank account with those of other women in my age bracket. Comparison truly is the thief of joy, isn't it, my friend?

As women of God, it is lethal to compare the impact that our lives have with the influence of well-known women of our generation. If I compare myself to a female politician, a beautiful celebrity, or a Grammy Award-winning musician, it is akin to comparing lions to kittens. The famous women of our generation who don't know Jesus as their Lord and Savior have large public platforms, but they do not have genuine power. These famous women are the kittens. But, as women who have opened our lives to the power of the Holy Spirit and the life-changing capacity of the Word of God, you and I have more power in our little fingers than the sum total of their lives will ever exhibit! We are the lions!

Platform does not equal power. You and I can be rich, dynamic demonstrations of what one ordinary woman is able to accomplish when she is filled with the awesome and dynamic power of God. Although we might not have high-profile public platforms, we are a threat to the kingdom of darkness because we have eternal power!

You plus God

Jeremiah had the power of God in his life, which means he was capable of much more than he first imagined, despite his youth and uncertainty. I believe that, as a woman filled with the power of the Holy Spirit and armed with the plans of God, you should actually do *more* of what scares you! Because you have Him, you have the wisdom, strength, endurance, and confidence to conquer mountains and to go where no woman has gone before! Therefore, when you have heard from God concerning your destiny and what He has appointed you to accomplish, do it even when your knees are shaking. Move forward in full assurance that the God who called you will never leave you or forsake you. (See Hebrews 13:5 NKJV.) He promises to always be with you. Even if your mouth is dry and your heart is pounding out of your chest, look the Father in the face and declare, "We've got this!"

There is no sin that marks a man or a woman as unfit for the redeeming power of Christ. And there is no human weakness or mistake that changes the plan of God for your life. Any mistake that you have made does not disqualify you for usefulness in His kingdom. Your past is not a regret; it is a lesson learned for the future. The only people whom the Father ever uses are broken, fallible men and women who have the extravagant ability to trust Him. You are never hopeless if you serve the God of all hope! Isn't it wonderful to know that you are allowed to be both a masterpiece and a work in progress, simultaneously?

Despite all of your valiant efforts to the contrary, you will never be able to talk God out of using you. You will never be able to convince Him that all of His brilliant preplanning, all of His incredible forethought, and all of His magnificent deliberations prior to your conception were a waste of His valuable time.

The greatest news to anyone who is dealing with a weakened, insecure life is this: God is with you. You don't have to perform, you don't have to achieve, and you certainly don't have to be credentialed when you have the Lord in you and with you. All that He desires is your acceptance of His will and plan. All that He expects is your cooperation with His Holy Spirit. The Lord promised to be with Jeremiah, and He has promised to be with you!

But the LORD said to me, "Do not say, 'I am a youth,' because everywhere I send you, you shall go, and all that I command you, you shall speak. Do not be afraid of them, for I am with you to deliver you," declares the LORD. —Jeremiah 1:7–8

As I ponder this conversation between God and His created son Jeremiah, which took place nearly three thousand years ago, I realize that the prophet dealt with some of the same fundamental issues that I do today. The Lord was giving Jeremiah directions, and yet this young man had to determine whether he would obey those words. Our individual calling only has the capacity to come to glorious fruition when we submit to the specific word of the Lord for our life. The fulfillment of God's purposes and plans for us depends upon our desire and follow-through to simply obey Him.

I see so much of myself in Jeremiah. Do you see yourself in this troubled and anxious young man as well? All Jeremiah could talk about was what he lacked and why God was unable to use him. But all God could talk about was His great plan for Jeremiah's life and the incredible things that he would be able to accomplish because the Lord was with him. Nothing has changed in three millennia, dear one. God is with you and has great plans for you. He simply desires for you to cooperate with Him.

For this reason, as you partner with God by walking in your destiny in Christ, make sure that you begin with the foundation of obedience. Before you speak or before you heal—obey Him. Before you write or before you compose—obey Him. Before you teach or before you invent—obey Him. Before you volunteer or before you start a ministry—obey Him.

Jeremiah was afraid and insecure. However, just as the Lord reminded him, we must remind ourselves that fear is always trumped by God's presence. Fear is an unnecessary emotion in life simply because the Lord is with us. When you hear fear knocking on the door of your heart, you can repeat to yourself God's promise that He will always be with you! This was a promise God made to the people of Israel through Moses long before Jeremiah was born:

Be strong and courageous, do not be afraid or tremble at them, for the LORD your God is the one who goes with you. He will not fail you or forsake you. —Deuteronomy 31:6

Moses told his successor, Joshua, the same thing:

The Lord is the one who goes ahead of you; He will be with you.
He will not fail you or forsake you. Do not fear or be dismayed.
—Deuteronomy 31:8

The same God who promised to be with the Israelites has promised to be with you. The same God who promised to be with Jeremiah has promised to be with you.

It Matters

After Jeremiah ceased talking back to God, the Lord reached down from heaven and gently touched the mouth of His humbled servant:

Then the Lord stretched out His hand and touched my mouth, and the Lord said to me, 'Behold, I have put My words in your mouth. See, I have appointed you this day over the nations and over the kingdoms...."
—Jeremiah 1:9–10

Do you remember what Jeremiah had said earlier? *"Behold, I do not know how to speak..."* (Jeremiah 1:6). It wasn't necessary for Jeremiah to speak his own human words, because the God who created him would provide even the words he needed to say during his lifetime. God called Jeremiah, He appointed him, He promised to be with him, and He provided for him—and the glory of it all is that He will do the same for you!

As you consider your calling in the mysterious yet certain purposes of God, it is vital for you to agree with His opinion of who you are and to declare what He says about your destiny. What you tell yourself about yourself matters. What you tell yourself about your destiny and purpose matters.

The words that you speak concerning your calling reveal more than just the issues that are in your heart—they have the propensity to either propel you or paralyze you. Why would we speak out of frustration, unbelief, or negativity when we are given the opportunity to speak like God speaks and to agree with His opinions? Why, indeed! Once you believe that you are who God says you are—at the very instant that you decide to agree that the Lord has called you for His pre-planned purposes—your words must reflect your belief system. This is an exciting moment in the life of a mere mortal! You are invited to think the thoughts of God concerning you, and you are commissioned to speak His powerful words over your existence.

God will always call us to do something that we are unable to do in our own strength or with human talents. He does not want us to develop a reliance on our own gifts, finances, education, or IQ. How wonderful of the Father to call us out of our comfort zones into His extravagant grace!

Isn't it interesting that although He planned for us and created us just the way we are for a reason, it is not about us or our strengths? God has intended for even our specific purposes to be about Him—and yet our personal callings are still evident in each of our lives. Always keep in mind that no one else in all of recorded history could have accomplished exactly what you and God are able to accomplish together. No one alive today can achieve what you and God are able to achieve together. And no one in the future will be able to do what you and God are able to do together! You and God together are unmatchable, unbeatable, and uncontainable!

⌒

"God will use whatever He wants to display His glory.
Heavens and stars. History and nations.
People and problems."
—*Max Lucado*

8

I Didn't Sign Up for the Battles!

When you understand the identity God has given to you and are finally ready to march into your destiny with His presence and power, the Lord then makes an astounding announcement: you are called to fight! You are no longer a reservist, but you have been drafted into active military duty in the army of God:

> *"They will fight against you, but they will not overcome you, for I am with you to deliver you," declares the* LORD. —Jeremiah 1:19

At the close of the stirring and life-altering conversation that Jeremiah had with his Creator, the Lord said, in effect, "Oh, by the way, Jerry, just as I assigned to you a specific identity and a unique calling, I have assigned to you personal battles. But don't worry, Jerry, my boy—you are going to win every battle that you fight in My strength! Attaboy, Jerry! And, I promise to stay with you and deliver you from every strategy of the enemy. It's all good, Jerry; it's all good!"

Can you imagine this scene? Can you picture God looking at Jeremiah with confident assurance in His eternal eyes and informing him that it wasn't all going to be roses and white picket fences along his life's journey? That there would be some atrociously difficult days ahead for this angst-driven young man? And do you realize that God has the same information for you concerning the days of your life? Jesus said nearly the exact words to His band of brothers during His tenure on earth:

These things I have spoken to you, so that in Me you may have peace. In the world you have tribulation, but take courage; I have overcome the world.   —John 16:33

Our destiny is certainly filled with amazing purpose, answered prayers, and dreams that come true, but it is also splattered with the fiery darts of the enemy. You have been empowered to batter the gates of hell—and they will come down! (See Matthew 16:18.) You got the job! You have been assigned, in the plans and purposes of God for your life, to defy the enemy and to obliterate the evil plans that he has intended.

It's true! While we all have personal callings and incredible destinies when we partner with the Lord, I also believe that He assigns battles to us. In the decades of my life, I have been assigned several battles that have threatened to distract me, confuse me, and derail me, but instead I have used them as a springboard for greater ministry.

In my late twenties, I ached to enlarge our family, which then consisted of two adorable, lively little boys. My husband and I deeply desired to raise a family of world-changing warriors for the kingdom of God. I became pregnant, but lost the baby at twelve weeks. Then I became pregnant again, but lost the second baby at fifteen weeks. My doctor was hopeful that I would be able to carry a baby to term, and so, after the appropriate amount of time had passed to ensure my health and that of the baby, I became pregnant once more—but lost the third baby at sixteen weeks.

My brilliant doctor at the Duke Fertility Center was convinced that if they watched me closely enough, I would be able to carry a baby to forty weeks, but after I conceived again, the fourth baby died in my womb at nineteen weeks. Although I was fighting depression with every cell in my body, I did become pregnant once again, only to lose the fifth baby at sixteen weeks. I was in the thick of the battle, and I hated every minute of it. Now, let me quickly assure you that I don't believe God caused the babies to die in my womb. However, I do believe that He was with me and that He allowed me the honor of fighting this wicked enemy known as "infertility."

And then, after losing five babies, I stopped ovulating, and the possibility of even becoming pregnant again was growing dimmer with every passing month. The years went by. Although my arms were empty of a newborn and my emotions were unstable, my heart was resolved. I knew that I knew that I knew that I was born to raise a large family for the glory of God, and so my husband and I continued to fight in this arena of battle.

Eventually, I was able to become pregnant three more times and carry each pregnancy to term. Our family grew from our two precious boys to include another dear son and two beautiful daughters. However, this did not happen without focused warfare and unshakable resolve. My five children on earth have made me a very happy woman, but my five babies in heaven have revolutionized this formerly depressed woman into a defiantly joyful Christian.

I am now able to pray with power for women who deal with infertility and to stand in strong faith with them as the arrows of the enemy fly around us. Infertility is no match for this woman who knows who she is in Christ, and also knows that she has been born with purpose and destiny. I have received literally hundreds of e-mails from women who have struggled with infertility whom I have prayed for, and who are now joyful mothers of children, either by birth or by adoption.

Not Just One Battle

I believe the stronghold of depression is another battlefront to which I have been assigned. When I was combating infertility, depression called my name loudly! I sank into a black hole that threatened to consume my very existence. The only thing I did well during that season of my life was that I continued to mother my two young sons with creativity and kindness. I barely cooked, I rarely cleaned, and I cried more than I smiled. It was hellacious to drag myself out of bed in the mornings. Depression had come in to conquer and to destroy.

During that period of my life, I also developed an overwhelming addiction. It wasn't an addiction to alcohol, over-the-counter medication, sleep aids, or eating. It was an addiction to the Word of God! The Bible delivered me from that inky black emotional sinkhole before my circumstances ever changed.

Today, I have the power and the testimony to encourage others in their valiant battle against depression. In His omniscience, the Lord knew that He had placed within me, a formerly depressed Christian, the supernatural resolve to help women live in a healthy place emotionally, regardless of their circumstances. Although I am unable to change anyone's situation in life, I can help them, through the principles found in the Bible, to process their circumstances in a joyful and hopeful manner.

The devil has found, time after time, that he is messing with the wrong woman when He messes with me! This is simply because I believe what the Bible says about me and I concur with God in His opinion of my life. I am not afraid of a battle or two this side of heaven because I know that I have been preprogrammed for victory!

Knowing that you have been assigned to tear down demonic strongholds and conquer oppression is what makes the hard stuff in life both worthwhile and meaningful. The battles that you face are nothing to shrink back from, nor are they a reason for dread. Battles should bring out the very best in you! Battles should cultivate the power of God in your life. Perhaps your battles were meant to be your finest hour! It could be that when you find yourself in the middle of a devastating situation, as Esther in the Bible did, the Holy Spirit will whisper in your ear, "You have been born for such a moment as this!" (See Esther 4:14.)

"I'm not sure we do a woman justice when she endures something brutal, and we chalk it up to strength. Sometimes people with no strength at all emerge from a horrifying season. They used all the might they had just to hold on to Jesus. And He was enough. In their weakness,
He was strong."
—*Beth Moore*, Children of the Day

9

When the Hard Stuff Becomes the Good Stuff

We all long for our destinies to be happily filled to the brim with glad days and sunshine. There's a human default that only wants the good stuff in life; we never want to wrestle with the bad. Most of us, when we see a storm headed in the direction of our unsuspecting lives, want to run to the nearest daisy field that we can find! However, I believe that our true moments of destiny and purpose are discovered amid the rocky places, the storm fronts, and the battlefields of life.

Now, let me assure you once more that I do not believe God sends trouble into the lives of His children, but I do believe we live in a fallen world and are often caught in the crossfire of the enemy. Our Father is so magnificent, so benevolent, and so powerful that He is well able to take what the enemy meant for evil and turn it into something wonderful! (See Genesis 50:20.)

I have a well-worn copy of the beloved, classic devotional *Streams in the Desert*, which belonged to my grandfather and then to my father. I was blessed to be bequeathed this family heirloom. I often turn the pages with wonder as I recall the two men before me who used this book for daily encouragement. I gaze with longing and endless interest at the notes and markings that cover each page. One of the quotes from this devotional, which has become most precious to me as I travel the rocky road of life, is this: "All of the tomorrows of our life have to pass before Him before they can get to us."[6]

Be Strong

When the enemy dares to invade your life with his fiery darts, when you meet the vicious crossfire, and when your life explodes right in front of you, rather than giving in to out-of-control emotions like fear or panic, you must purpose in your heart to be strong in the Lord! Preparing ahead of time for these assaults is essential:

Finally, be strong in the Lord and in the strength of His might. Put on the full armor of God, so that you will be able to stand firm against the schemes of the devil. For our struggle is not against flesh and blood, but against the rulers, against the powers, against the world forces of this darkness, against the spiritual forces of wickedness in the heavenly places. —Ephesians 6:10–12

"*Put on the full armor of God, so that you will be able to stand firm against* **the schemes of the devil**." The Father is not the only one who has purposes and plans for your magnificent life. Satan, the enemy of your soul, has specific goals in mind to thwart you, in hopes of furthering his dastardly cause.

The Greek word translated "*schemes*" in the above verse refers to an orderly or technical plan that has been established by cunning arts, deceit, or trickery. Make no mistake about it, dear friend, the devil does have a plan for your life!

---

6. F. B. Meyer, quoted in *Streams in the Desert* by Mrs. Charles E. Cowman (Cowman Publications, Inc., 1953), 23 (entry for January 14).

He has been scheming across the centuries, and his intent is to use your life as the means through which he can rob God of the glory He deserves. God's plan, however, is to show His magnificent glory through your life!

Your heavenly Father's purpose is to give you *"a future and a hope"* (Jeremiah 29:11), while the enemy seeks to bring you calamity on every side and in every season. The Lord wants you to live an abundant life filled with joy, hope, and peace, but the devil wants to steal your joy, kill your hope, and destroy your peace. (See John 10:10.) In fact, the enemy's intention for your life is for you to look for joy in all the wrong places and to grope for temporary pleasures instead of eternal rewards.

As a child of God, when the enemy comes against you, your prevailing instinct and first reaction should be to declare, "I am *'strong in the Lord and in the strength of His might'*!" So many women resort to fear or panic when faced with the schemes of the enemy. Instead of clothing themselves with God's power at this decisive moment, they turn to wine or chocolate or shopping or tears. As God's beloved creation, made in His image, you must choose to be a resplendent woman who refuses to whine and resists worry. You must make a commitment to partner with the Holy Spirit to reveal the glory of God—no matter how fierce the battle may become. Be a significant woman who defiantly chooses to worship as the flames are whipping around you! It is in that glorious defiance that you will experience God's sweet and comforting presence.

Whenever I find myself in a vicious battle with Satan, I quickly remind myself that warfare always surrounds the birth of a miracle, so I am in a wonderful position!

A Spiritual Truths Review

Before we march forward in our divine camouflage to fight against the enemy of our souls, let's pause for just a moment to review these indispensable spiritual truths:

+ God's plan for your life is a definite one, and He imagined all that you would become. He created you and strategically placed you to live today in the blueprint of history.

+ Your heavenly Father has dreamed about you and declared that you are a masterpiece of His image and likeness!

+ You were totally loved by God before you were in your mother's womb. You were not a surprise, and you are not just a "number."

+ All of the heavenly host stood to their feet and roared with thunderous approval as you marched onto the stage of history.

+ Not one single thing comes into your life that does not have some eternal bearing on God's purpose for you in your own generation.

+ You are here now, in the first part of the twenty-first century, to give God glory every day and in every situation.

+ Your life is a perfect fit for the glory of the Father. It is meant to be a show-and-tell of God's joy, hope, and peace, no matter what your circumstances may be.

+ The enemy also has a plan for your life. He has watched you and plotted to stamp your life with calamity and emptiness. His one driving purpose is to steal the glory that you, as a daughter of God, were created to shine at your moment in history. He has schemes to remove that glory from your life.

+ The enemy endeavors to discourage you so that you will no longer have the desire to tell the story of Jesus with your life. He does this especially when you are in a rocky stretch, where he hopes that you will "*become weary in doing good*" (Galatians 6:9 NIV).

+ The enemy's diabolical scheme is to get you to fall flat on your beautiful face when life is hard! But you must always remember that you, dear one, are here to reveal Jesus with your life!

A Chocolate Cake and You

As women of the twenty-first century who are intent on discovering our destiny and purpose, there is one familiar but extraordinary verse that we must keep at the forefront of our thought processes:

God causes all things to work together for good to those who love God, to those who are called according to His purpose.

—Romans 8:28

I am not a great cook by any stretch of the imagination, and the stark truth is that I have never baked a chocolate cake from scratch! Never! Rarely do I even buy a cake mix to turn into something yummy that will thrill my family's taste buds. No, the way that I create a culinary celebration for those whom I love is by marching into a bakery and choosing the most delectable concoction that I spy in the display case.

However, I will tell you that I have watched my little Irish grandmother bake many chocolate cakes from scratch, so I know what goes into that delicious and rich confection. If you or I were to bake a chocolate cake from scratch, we would need flour, lard or shortening, baking soda, baking powder, salt, eggs, sugar, buttermilk, and unsweetened cocoa powder.

Now, let me just be quick to inform you that any one of those ingredients, on their own, could make you violently sick if you ate it in large proportions, right? Who wants to eat a cup of shortening or even a tablespoon of baking soda? Who sits around thinking, "I'd really like to eat two raw eggs for dinner, followed by three cups of flour!"?

Yet, when all of the above ingredients are carefully mixed together in proportion, poured into a greased pan, and then placed in the oven for the designated time, a delicious, irresistible chocolate cake emerges! God, who is an expert at creating a blessed life and who thinks about you without ceasing, is able to take all of your circumstances, both delightful and difficult, and gently mix them together with His arm of love. Then, because He has oiled your life with the amazing Holy Spirit, when the heat of circumstances are turned up to blistering temperatures by the enemy, it will serve not to destroy you but to turn you into something divinely magnificent that you could never become on your own.

According to Romans 8:28, God has been to your future, and it is good because He is there, and He is good all the time! Doesn't that comfort you as you walk through a difficult season? Remind yourself daily that nothing is allowed to touch your life that is without purpose for your generation. Nothing is allowed to attack you that God is unable to work for your good and His glory!

Enriching the Unshakable Kingdom

During His tenure on planet earth, Jesus Himself struggled with the purposes and plans of the Father during heartbreaking moments. One time, while He was wrestling with His purpose, His human pain was so intense that He even sweat great drops of blood. (See Luke 22:44.) It is not a sin to struggle with the circumstances of our lives, as long as we struggle on our knees. It is not a sign of weakness to wrestle with disappointment, as long as we wrestle in the throne room of God.

And [Jesus] *withdrew from them about a stone's throw, and He knelt down and began to pray, saying, "Father, if You are willing, remove this cup from Me; yet not My will, but Yours be done."*

—Luke 22:41–42

The Greek word translated *"willing"* in this verse comes from the same root word, *boule'*, that is translated as *"purpose"* in Acts 13:36, where it says that *"David…served the purpose of God in his own generation."* On this stormy night of the soul in the garden of Gethsemane, Jesus went to His good, good Father and entreated Him to reconsider His plans and purposes. He begged His Dad, in essence, "Father, in Your well-thought-out plans, desires, and strategies for Me, if You could let this particular circumstance pass Me by, please let it happen. However, I know that You have planned My mission on earth from eternity, and I only want what You want. You know My eternal purpose, Father, so whatever is wrapped up in Your plans, let it come. Whatever is not in Your purpose, let it pass me by."

Are you brave enough, humble enough, and willing enough to pray the same prayer that Jesus did the night before Calvary? God loved His Son Jesus, and yet He still allowed Him to experience the agony of the cross.

Why would a loving Father allow His precious child to go through such suffering and pain? Why, indeed!

I believe that in the case of God's plan for the life of His Son, it was because the pain and suffering of Jesus would serve a greater good. Jesus's death and resurrection brought glory to the Father and enriched the kingdom of God. Perhaps that is why, even though God the Father could enable us to circumvent disappointments, wretched circumstances, and dire straits, He allows us to walk through them. Perhaps His goal in our lives is to serve a greater good than our own human comfort can deliver. The God of the universe is certainly wise and powerful enough to bring glory to His name when our world falls apart. Perhaps He knows that He can enrich His unshakable kingdom by allowing His power to flow through us when all else fails from a human standpoint.

God can work anything—anything at all—for our good and His glory. What we might consider horrible from our limited viewpoint, we can be assured heaven views as valuable from a different perspective entirely. Heaven sees our pain as an opportunity for a miraculous intervention of God! Heaven sees our searing disappointment as a moment when God's goodness will overpower the evil ways of the enemy.

I have gone through many experiences in life—both good and bad, easy and hard. I have found unending happiness during the sunny, cheerful days of my existence. However, I have also discovered joy and even purpose when my life has been violently torn apart by trying circumstances in this fallen world. I can assure you that when your life is exploding in front of your eyes, there will come a day when you will say with me, "Jesus is more powerful than anything that has ever caused me pain."

"While it looks like things are out of control, behind the scenes there is a God who hasn't surrendered His authority."
—A. W. Tozer

10

Joe and I

My favorite Old Testament character is a young man by the name of Joseph. You might remember him as the seventeen-year-old who was bold enough to tell his brothers the extraordinary prophetic dreams that he'd been having concerning his future and destiny. Joseph was his father's favorite son, and he had been given a rainbow-colored tunic by his doting dad that showcased his number one status in the family.

His brothers were so insanely jealous of their younger brother that, one day, they stripped his tunic off him, threw him into a pit, and then sold him to a passing caravan of Midianite traders. These traders knew that they could make a pretty penny off of this good-looking, well-fed young man, and so they sold Joseph into slavery in Egypt.

Joseph served in the household of an Egyptian officer and gained great favor there. The Bible indicates that in this foreign home, under adverse conditions, Joseph knew the presence of the Lord as never before: *"The Lord was with Joseph, so he succeeded in everything he did as he served in the home of his Egyptian master*" (Genesis 39:2 NLT). The Egyptian officer's wife, however, noted how handsome Joseph was, and she had her devious eye upon him. She began to sexually harass him, and he was forced to flee from the home. The wife then accused Joseph of making sexual advances against her (rather than the other way around), and he was put into prison. Yet, even in the filth and confines of that jail, Joseph gained the appreciation and favor of those in charge, and he knew, once again, that the Lord was with him. (See verses 21–22.)

Joseph acquired a reputation in prison for having the unusual, God-given ability to interpret dreams. One night, Pharaoh, the ruler of Egypt, had a dream that troubled him greatly. Joseph was called up from prison to interpret Pharaoh's dream, and he gave this earthly authority figure God's insight into the matter. When the ruler realized what an extraordinary young man Joseph was, he gave him a position equivalent to prime minister of the entire nation of Egypt!

Joseph, being inspired by wisdom from God, actually saved the Egyptian people from decimation with a program to provide food for them during seven years of devastating, widespread famine. While other nations were starving, the people under Joseph's authority continued to thrive and even be well-fed.

Meanwhile, Joseph's family back in Canaan was feeling the effects of this severe famine. His brothers traveled to Egypt to try to barter for food, but although Joseph recognized them, they didn't recognize him. The last time they had seen Joseph, he had been a gangly teenager, and now he had grown to full manhood and was an impressive leader, with the appearance of an Egyptian. (See Genesis 37, 39–49.)

It's All Good

At the end of this story, as he looked into the now wrinkled and aged faces of his older brothers, this is what Joseph kindly told them: *"As for you, you meant evil against me, but God meant it for good in order to bring about this present result, to preserve many people alive"* (Genesis 50:20).

Do you remember the Hebrew word *machashabah*, which we noted in chapter 5 of this book when we lingered over Jeremiah 29:11, *"'For I know the* **plans** *that I have for you,' declares the* Lord, *'plans for welfare and not for calamity to give you a future and a hope'"*? *Machashabah* is the word that is rendered as "plans" in this verse in many translations. However, we learned that this word means so much more than mere "plans." It can also signify "thought," "device," "intention," "purpose," "invention," "imagination," or "artistic work."

Our favorite Egyptian ruler, Joseph, used a term that came from the root word *machashab*, when he said, *"You* **meant** *evil against me, but God* **meant** *it for good."*

Are you shouting yet? God can take anything that anyone throws at us, no matter how evil or abusive it might be, and He can "machashab" it for our good! God will never allow anything into our lives that He is not able to "machashab" for a greater good and for a redemptive plan. He is able to morph the schemes and plans of the enemy into something incredibly wonderful. That is your destiny, my friend! You serve a God who can "machashab" human pain, disappointment, mistreatment, and wretched abuse into something glorious that will *"preserve many people alive"*!

This truth causes my heart to overflow with wonder and gratitude, and I want to share with you again how God has used disappointments and pain in my life for His redemptive plans:

+ He took the loss of my five little babies and "machashabed" it for good. That is why I am now able to pray in faith for other women who are in the midst of the grief of infertility and to bring them the comfort of the Lord.

+ He "machashabed" seven years of clinical depression, and now I am a woman who is defiantly joyful and able to minister to others who have been afflicted by depression. God is using me in my generation, sending me to a world filled with women who are battling this dark malaise of the soul. He has told me, "Carol, this is your purpose!"

+ He "machashabed" my horrific battle with cancer so that I am now able to boldly pray for women to be healed in Jesus's name. I can walk into the offices of oncologists and surgeons with hope in my heart and know that I have been sent there strategically by the hand of God to encourage other women who are facing this archenemy.

Father Knows Best

For a life event to pass God's purpose test, you can be assured that the purpose must exceed the pain. The enemy can think that he is doing something dastardly and evil in your life, but when you allow God to enter the tragic scene, your heavenly Father will use the situation for a greater good and for the saving of many lives! I would rather go through pain and allow God to use it for His purposes of bringing other people to Him than not go through it and allow a generation who does not know Him to go to hell. Wouldn't you?

Don't miss the extraordinary, miraculous promise that problems and pain can make us useful in the kingdom of God! When an ordinary woman chooses to be a vessel of glory at the worst moment of her life, she is walking in her chosen destiny. The hardest places in life can become holy places where God does His greatest work. As His beloved daughter, embrace every season of your life—even the seasons of pain and heartache. You serve a God who wastes nothing! Just as He did for my favorite Bible personality, Joseph, thousands of years ago, He can turn your pain into purpose. He can miraculously transform the bad into good—it is what our Father does best!

Comforters, Not Comfortable

Blessed be the God and Father of our Lord Jesus Christ, the Father of mercies and God of all comfort, who comforts us in all our afflic-tion so that we will be able to comfort those who are in any afflic-tion with the comfort with which we ourselves are comforted by God. —2 Corinthians 1:3–4

A vibrant but often ignored truth regarding our destiny this side of heaven is that we serve the *"God of all comfort"*! When you need comforting due to the stress of life, don't run to chocolate—run to Him! When you need comforting because your feelings have been hurt, don't go shopping—go to Him! When your life is in disarray from an onslaught of circumstances and you are not sure that you can go on, don't dissolve into tears—talk to Him! No one can comfort you like the Lord can. He is the *"God of all comfort."* Any comfort that is worth having is found in Him!

Why does the *"Father of mercies"* comfort His disheartened children? First, out of His everlasting love for us. And second, for the eternal purpose that now we can be qualified comforters in His name. That means that you, dear one, are a qualified comforter! You have been to the school of all comfort and have your degree in "Comforting Those in Affliction." That is a wonderful part of your destiny this side of heaven!

Who better to comfort a newly grieving widow than another widow who has also known the ache of grief, and has experienced the peace of God's presence? Who better to encourage a mother whose child is dealing with an addiction than another mother who has walked that same torturous road and found courage and strength in the Lord? Who better to hold the hand of a woman battling breast cancer than another woman with a scarred chest who has come through the pain, finding hope for the future? Who better to speak to a woman surprised by infertility than another woman who has experienced the same sense of emptiness and loss and been strengthened in faith? Who better to speak joy over a woman struggling with depression than another woman who has lived with this destructive malady, and been miraculously delivered from it through the power of God's Word? Who better?

"Brokenness is for a season,
but lessons from it are for a lifetime."
—*Priscilla Shirer*

11

He Needed One of You

Every morning, when your alarm clock rings, awakening you from the dead of sleep, you need to remind yourself, "I was strategically placed here at this time in history by my good, good Father for His glorious purposes and miraculous plans."

When you are dealing with discouragement or disappointment, remind yourself once again, "I was strategically placed here at this time in history by my good, good Father for His glorious purposes and miraculous plans."

When the children are whining, the laundry is piled high, and your husband forgot your birthday, remind yourself emphatically, "I was strategically placed here at this time in history by my good, good Father for His miraculous plans and glorious purposes."

When yet another New Year's Eve passes by and you are still not married, remind yourself, "I was strategically placed here at this time in history by my good, good Father for His miraculous plans and glorious purposes."

The Creator of the universe needed someone just like you alive in the world today to love the unlovable...to show joy to a dark, cold world...to bring peace into arguments and confusing situations...and to be kind at times when our culture is desolately cruel.

God needed someone just like you to be constantly optimistic in the face of frustrating circumstances...to hope when there is no natural reason for hope...and to show patience to obstinate and ornery people.

Because God needed you, He created you to reveal His heart in spite of disappointing people, overwhelming conditions, and devastating events. This, my friend, is your purpose.

The challenge is that, even though we are God's very own children, we have acquired too many genetic characteristics of the world and have forsaken the lavishly bestowed attributes of our loving Father.

The issue is that we would rather have it our way than His way.

The problem is that we would prefer to emote a selfish perspective on a situation than to exhibit the delightful fruit of the Spirit. We have mutated into an emotional counterfeit of who God intended for us to be. Our destiny in life should never be dictated by our emotions, but rather by His calling and fruit in our lives.

We were created by God to reveal His heart and to do His good works during this singular moment in all of recorded time. There is a lack of "Godness" on this earth, and so He sent us to bring His love and healing to a world in pain. We got the job, sister! It is our grand destiny!

Chicken Doo-Doo, Green Paint, and George Washington

When my mom and dad married in the 1950s, they were given an old, beat-up dresser by my father's parents. This dresser had been in the chicken shed of the family farm for many decades, but my well-meaning paternal grandmother thought that my parents could put it to good use in their eclectic, newlywed home. The chest of drawers was covered with years of dust, chicken doo-doo, and countless feathers from generations of hens.

My grandmother tried cleaning it up but found it impossible, so she just covered the grotesque residue with a coat of ugly, pea-green paint.

This bumpy, green dresser sat in our upstairs hallway for all of my childhood. We used it as a storage chest for dress-up clothes and Tinkertoys. In the top drawer, there were stacks of construction paper, hundreds of broken Crayola crayons, and numerous permanent markers with no caps to them.

The chest of drawers remained that putrid shade of green until I left for college in the summer of 1973. At that point, my mom decided to finally have the ugly paint removed, in hopes that she might pass the dresser on to me someday. She took it to a family friend, Mr. Cianfrini, who had established a refinishing business in his garage in his retirement years. She often took pieces of furniture to Mr. Cianfrini, who restored scratched and stained wood to its original glory.

My mom dropped the hideous dresser off on her way to work one morning, and the very next day, Mr. C. called and told her to come by and pick it up. She couldn't imagine that he had finished such a damaged piece of furniture so quickly and asked him how he had completed it in a mere twenty-four hours.

In his thick Italian accent, Mr. C. explained that as he took a thorough look at the olive-green dresser and then researched its features in a book that identified expensive antiques, he realized that this piece of furniture had been made during the Revolutionary War and that it was a priceless antique. Mr. C. said that it was reminiscent of furniture made for George Washington himself! He refused to touch it and encouraged my mother to take it to a professional craftsman. He said that it was worth tens of thousands of dollars...potentially, even more.

Mom insisted that Mr. C. was the only one that she would trust to restore this unique piece of history. She knew that whatever he touched, he did so with loving care. It took Mr. C. months to painstakingly refurbish the dresser to its original condition. Gently, oh so gently, he removed the horrid paint...and then the grime...and finally the stains. After this, he buffed it and varnished it—restoring it to its intended beauty.

We are like that dresser, my friend. We were designed by our wonderful Creator to be valued and cared for. But, instead, we have chosen to live in the chicken coop of life, and it has covered us with doo-doo, feathers, and decades of dirt. On top of the pain that has been clinging to our life for far too long, some well-meaning, self-help guru has painted us an unnatural and unbecoming hue. God desires to remove all of that ugly pain and to slowly, gently, and lovingly restore us to the natural beauty of His creation. Will you allow Him to do that? Will you remain in His presence long enough for Him to clean you up so that He can show you off? Your life is not your own, you know, but you have been created in God's image to be part of His plans at this time in history.

Hanging Out with Dad

For we are His workmanship, created in Christ Jesus for good works, which God prepared beforehand so that we would walk in them. —Ephesians 2:10

The Greek word translated *"workmanship"* in this well-known verse, written by Paul and the Holy Spirit, depicts someone putting forth their fullest creative abilities in order to achieve something. God did not create you for chicken doo-doo, discarded feathers, or decades of grime. He designed you as a masterwork of the rarest and most valuable kind.

Think about that for a minute! The same artistic Genius who made the redwood forests, Victoria Falls, and the White Cliffs of Dover has placed us at the very top of His creative resume! I love this quote, which I repeat at the end of this chapter: "Isn't it astounding that the same God who created mountains and oceans and galaxies looked at the world and thought that it needed one of you, too?"

I often enjoy imagining what actually happened at biblical events and have been known to invent conversations spoken between people whose names frequent the pages of Scripture. One day, as I was meditating on the stunning implication that I am the highest work of art that the Father ever created—as are all His children—I wove the following imaginary yet powerful conversation between God the Father and Jesus the Son in the fabric of my brain.

Let's suppose for a moment that Jesus is hanging out with His Dad during the period of time that we know as "creation." God the Father, in magnificent, paternal fashion, exclaims, "Look, Son!" And with those two words, He hurls the Grand Canyon into visible existence.

The Son respectfully responds with a teasing yet proud grin on His face, "Come on, Dad! Is that really the best that You can do?" As the Father's eyes sparkle from the loving challenge, He says with joy, "How about this?" And He immediately forms the glaciers of Alaska, causing them to spring up in the cold, arctic waters.

Jesus, who loves to partner with His Dad in everything, then reacts by exclaiming, "Dad, that's pretty good! But I think that You can do even better than that!"

I envision the Father laying one finger beside His nose and tapping it there gently while immersed in deep, creative thought. Then, He suddenly turns to face His Son and declares, "Let there be fjords!" And in that one magnificent and miraculous moment, fjords are flung across the Scandinavian expanse.

The Son high-fives His infinitely creative Father and enthusiastically says, "Dad, that is so impressive! You know what? You are really good at what You do! But come on now—You are God! You must have something else fantastic up Your miraculous sleeve!" The Father grins at His faith-filled, divine Son and says, "You're on! What this world needs right now are the Rocky Mountains!" With that declaration, the earth rumbles, and just to the west of the Great Plains of America rise the towering and majestic Rocky Mountains.

Jesus is nearly rendered speechless by the "purple mountain majesties" that have sprung up where before there had only been flatlands. However, when He gains His composure through the help of the Holy Spirit, He dares His Father one last time: "Wow, Dad! You are the best! There is no one like You! I love what You create! But I think that even You can do better than this!"

His Dad looks at what He has created by His words and by His power, and thoughtfully considers what has not yet been done. I imagine Him looking far into the distance of time and wondering what He could do to impact history with His heart and His compassion. And, in the quietness of possibility, God the Father thinks of you! You were fashioned in the heart and mind of God to be the crowning achievement of all that He has ever produced by His power. You are God's first-time-in-forever creation!

Our Life in Christ

God created you in Christ so that you would not live a life separate from Him. He created you to live and breathe and have your very being in Him. (See Acts 17:28.) What a grand life! He is the One who is Life incarnate, and we get to live our lives in Him. Have you discovered yet that there is no life apart from Christ? In Christ, and in Christ alone, we can live exuberantly, fully, enthusiastically, and with eternal purpose.

"For we are His workmanship, created in Christ Jesus for good works, which God prepared beforehand so that we would walk in them." Ephesians 2:10 states exactly why you were born—you were *"created in Christ Jesus for good works."* Now, let me be quick to state that these good works don't save you from sin and death, but they do accomplish God's purposes and bring fulfillment to you on planet earth. The good works that you were fashioned to do are an important part of your job description and are a benefit to the world in which you live.

The Greek word translated *"prepared beforehand"* means "to fit up in advance," "to ordain before," or "to prepare beforehand in mind and purpose, that is, to decree." You have been created to excel in all that is good and useful. Before you were born, God spent time contemplating all that you would become, and He planned that your life would be valuable to His kingdom during your moment on earth. He prepared a list of specific assignments, making sure that they would be a perfect fit for you!

Romans 9:23 tells us that God bestowed *"the riches of His glory upon vessels of mercy, which He **prepared beforehand for glory**."* Those *"vessels of mercy"* are us. In the context of this verse, *"prepared beforehand"* refers to our being prepared for glory: "for whom [God] appointed glory beforehand (that is, from eternity), and, accordingly, rendered them fit to receive it."

Don't overlook this spiritual principle! Your life is a perfect fit for the glory of God. God decreed, for all of His creation to hear, "I chose her to carry My glory!" You are the carrier of the DNA of God's glory, and it is up to you to reflect it on both good days and hard days.

The Lord has announced that you are the most profound, priceless, and amazing miracle that has ever been created. He couldn't do better than you! Your life represents His finest moment. And because you are so valuable to His plan, He placed you in the safest and most powerful place He could find: He placed you *"in Christ Jesus."*

My friend, as a woman of the twenty-first century, you have been granted the life of Jesus, the healing power of Jesus, and the authority of Jesus. You have been bequeathed the strength of Jesus, the wisdom of Jesus, and the joy of Jesus's presence! And you have been given all of that, in the love of God, because you have an exciting and exacting job description:

+ There are people to pray for...continents to visit...missionaries to send out...books to write...people to encourage...and children to love.

+ There are inventions to be created...cures to be discovered...songs to be composed...and melodies to be sung.

+ There are meals to be cooked...notes to be written...hugs to be offered...smiles to be given...and laughter to resound through the rooms of your home.

+ There are walks to be taken...diapers to be changed...artwork to be created...and sweaters to be knitted.

+ There are holidays to be celebrated...cookies to be baked...meetings to be attended...and cantankerous people to be loved.

+ There are gifts to be given...phone calls to be made...hands to be held...and sunsets to be enjoyed!

Dear friend, as you walk in God's unspeakably splendid plans, you will miraculously find that your calling in life is being fulfilled. You will discover the unmatchable and unbeatable objective of living every day in Christ. You will celebrate the purpose of pointing other searchers to Him.

You have a choice: Are you going to acquiesce to the schemes of the enemy, permitting him to direct your life? Or will you walk out your extraordinary life in Christ Jesus? Will you go down the rocky road of compromises and trespasses or will you keep in stride with the incredibly good plans that God has for you? Will you fight the wrong battles or will you wage your divinely assigned battles? What will you do?

When you discover the very reason for which you were created and give yourself to that reason, then you, my friend, will reveal the glory of God in your life! God has known all along a fact that you and I may have ignored: when we find our passion in life, it will not be "work" to us, but rather a means of great fulfillment. If you are still struggling to figure out your purpose, then simply discover your passion. I believe wholeheartedly that your passion will lead you directly into your purpose!

The Beginning of Amazing

Now you know why your life is so valuable to the kingdom of God! There is a world in pain that needs your voice, your time, your talents, your heart, and the fruit of the Holy Spirit that you exhibit in your life. People don't need your indifference, your tantrums, your volatile emotions, or even your opinions. What they desperately need is the Jesus who is in you. They need the glory that you were created to carry. They need the love of the Father that can only be revealed through the one and only you!

In the book of 2 Corinthians, we find some powerful and fitting verses that, with your newfound understanding of your purpose, will hold even greater impact for your common yet uncommon life:

But we have this treasure in earthen vessels, so that the surpassing greatness of the power will be of God and not from ourselves; we are afflicted in every way, but not crushed, perplexed but not despairing, persecuted but not forsaken, struck down, but not destroyed; always carrying about in the body the dying of Jesus, so that the life of Jesus also may be manifested in our body. For we who live are constantly being delivered over to death for Jesus' sake, so that the life of Jesus also may be manifested in our mortal flesh. So death works in us, but life in you. —2 Corinthians 4:7–12

The difficult assignment that the Holy Spirit has given to you is actually the easiest thing you have ever done! That is because, when you determine to be who God created you to be and to partner with Him in the display of His glory, you will certainly change the world just by being the "you" that you were designed to be. When life is hard…reveal Jesus. When times are outrageously difficult…be a blessing. When you are not sure that you can go on another day…hold God's hand and go on anyway.

When certain verses in the Bible seem too difficult for me to understand, I often try to read them in a different Scripture version or paraphrase. Although a paraphrase is certainly not a word-for-word translation of the original language, I have discovered that it can often breathe new life into a passage for me, helping me to apply it to my life in a more exact manner. Therefore, as we close this portion of the book, let's reread our job description for the times when life is difficult, as found in *The Message* paraphrase:

If you only look at us, you might well miss the brightness. We carry this precious Message around in the unadorned clay pots of our ordinary lives. That's to prevent anyone from confusing God's incomparable power with us. As it is, there's not much chance of that. You know for yourselves that we're not much to look at. We've been surrounded and battered by troubles, but we're not demoralized; we're not sure what to do, but we know that God knows what to do; we've been spiritually terrorized, but God hasn't left our side; we've been thrown down, but we haven't broken. What they did to Jesus, they do to us—trial and torture; mockery and

murder; what Jesus did among them, He does in us—He lives!
Our lives are at constant risk for Jesus' sake, which makes Jesus'
life all the more evident in us. While we're going through the worst,
you're getting in on the best!   —2 Corinthians 4:7–12

"Isn't it astounding that the same God who created
mountains and oceans and galaxies looked at the world and
thought that it needed one of you too?"
—*Unknown author*

PART THREE

You Are...a Woman of Glorious Identity

12

Nice to Meet You, Self!

Self-esteem is comprised of two potentially lethal words: *self* and *esteem*. When these two words are placed innocently together with the olive branch of the hyphen between them, the battle begins in the soul of a woman. In its simplest reduction, the concept of "self-esteem" is a mere enigma to us. Yet, when it is considered in the extreme, it has the potential of blowing up the very psyche of a woman who is trying to live in Christlike humility but doesn't fully understand how she has been made in the image of the Creator God.

This explosive word suggests a plethora of questions with no easy answers.

Am I even supposed to esteem myself? If so, to what degree?

When does self-esteem become pride?

Am I supposed to constantly put myself down in order to make others look better? Isn't that the godly thing to do?

Is it humbler, and somehow holier, to remind yourself daily that you are merely a "worm" and that there is no good thing in you?

Is it prideful to feel good about how you look or about what you do?

Is it narcissism to dream about your potential in life?

Is it more Christlike to beat that pretentious ego down into a mere pulp of itself?

How Self-Esteem Develops

Confusion about our identity doesn't usually begin in adulthood. Our self-esteem is not birthed from only one place in life or from one circumstance we experience. It is conceived in our home life during our childhood and is added to as we meet and interact with people in various situations in life. However, the foundation of our self-esteem can always be traced back to the formative, growing years of infancy, childhood, and adolescence. When we compare ourselves with others, subconsciously finding ourselves lacking in either looks, smarts, or ability, questions such as these can discharge in rapid-fire succession:

I was always chosen last for the kickball team at school—how can anyone possibly like me?

I've never had a date—will anyone ever love me the way I am?

My parents never said, "I love you"—I guess that I am unlovable in every way, shape, and form. If my own parents don't even appreciate me, how will anyone else acknowledge my very existence?

My second-grade teacher told me that I would never amount to anything. She was right, wasn't she?

Even my best friend in the eighth grade gossiped about me. Does that mean that everyone talks about me behind my back? Does anyone ever say anything kind about me?

Everyone Struggles

As a pastor's wife for over forty years and someone who has mentored and ministered to women for nearly half a century, I can assure you that you are not alone in your internal conflict over the meaning of that dreaded compound word *self-esteem*.

Stay-at-home moms struggle with self-esteem largely due to the lies that our culture promotes about women who have chosen to be full-time homemakers. They feel insignificant as they clean toilets and read endless fairy tales to their children. Mothers often wonder if they have wasted the most valuable years of their lives wiping noses, making grilled cheese sandwiches, and folding mountains of laundry.

At the other end of the life spectrum, empty-nesters have a vicious battle with that monster word *self-esteem* too. Women whose children have left home now wonder what their purpose in life is. Their homes may now be immaculate, but dinnertime is abysmally quiet, and they wonder if they will ever do anything as significant again as raising a family.

Widows are also engaged in volatile warfare with the onslaught of thoughts that question their worth. Women who have lost their life's mate often assume that their best days are behind them. They falsely believe that they are now defined by memories rather than by potential. Widows often have a difficult time believing the promise of Scripture that your latter years can indeed be better than your former. (See Job 8:7; Haggai 2:9.)

Single women struggle valiantly, but often futilely, in their attempt to combat the giant of insignificance and to win the war of self-respect and dignity. Whether you have never been married or have been divorced, feeling rejected by men is a heavy weight to carry as you try to step into a place of healthy self-esteem. Single women in their lonely and understandable pain need to be reminded often that you don't need to have a significant other in order to lead a significant life. If you perpetually wrestle with your value as a woman based upon how men respond to you, it will greatly influence how you view yourself. This opens the door to mocking thoughts that are at once ridiculous and valid:

Will a man ever desire me?

Will a man ever kiss me? Hold me? Treasure me?

If I had any value as a woman at all, a man would have surely chosen me by now. Because I have been rejected by men, I have no value...none whatsoever.

One of the saddest commentaries of our society is that little girls are forming their self-worth at ten to twelve years of age based upon how little boys treat them. Preadolescent girls are also defining their worth by the false images that television presents, by the lyrics of songs they listen to on repeat, and by how they feel they measure up in comparison to their peers on social media. This situation is commencing earlier and earlier in the lives of little girls, who become insecure adolescents, who grow into anxious women.

Who Do You Think You Are?

As we begin to tackle these multiple self-esteem issues, one thing is vital: you need to answer this question for yourself: "Who do *you* think you are?" Throw away what the world may say about you, what your parents believed about you, how men have treated you, and how your friends have assessed your personal worth as a human being. Who do *you* think you are?

Your voice is the one voice that truly matters, so you must have a healthy and whole view of who you are. Otherwise, you will convince yourself that you are someone whom you actually are not and will never be! As a woman, you will respond to others and react to circumstances based upon what you think about yourself.

If you believe that you are a woman of value, significance, and destiny, then that is how you will approach life. And you will treat others with value, importance, and worth regardless of how they have treated you.

Conversely, if you believe that you are a loser and that God forgot you when it came to talents, looks, and intelligence, then you will respond as a defeated human being. You will allow others to take advantage of you, and you will react out of emotions rather than out of purpose and destiny.

Let me just say that if you extract your identity from your "packaging," you will never unwrap the beautiful gift that you are to the world. If your mousy brown hair that is now turning gray, your too-large nose, or your extra-large shirts are setting your internal value, you will always be held back by inconsequential living. Your genetic features—whether gorgeous, mediocre, or forgettable by human standards—are only your outer covering. They are not the essence of who you are and should never be given the defining voice in your life. The powerful truth is this: You will never know yourself until you know yourself in God. You will never stand amazed at all of the gorgeous facets and intricate details that are uniquely yours until you stand amazed at your Creator and all that He is!

Who Does God Say That You Are?

As women who have attached our lives to the uncompromising truth found in the Word of God, we must acquire our self-esteem from that same Word. We must agree with God's assessment of our worth and true potential. As a vital and valuable woman alive at this moment in history, you must agree with who God says you are! If you don't agree with His description of you in the Bible, you will never walk in your destiny or be who God needs you to be in the world in which you live. If you erroneously mine for self-esteem from your parentage, your education, your marital status, or the number on the scale, you will not choose well in life. You might marry the wrong man or spend your money on wasteful things. It is possible that you will not even be the mother that your children need if you don't agree with God's assessment of your personhood.

Our actions tend to be directed by our belief system; therefore, what you believe is what you will become. The Bible says it like this: *"As [a person] thinks within himself, so he is"* (Proverbs 23:7).

You will never be able to live beyond who you think that you are. You will not break out of your own limitations unless you first break into who God says that you are. In order to discover who we are as women and who we were created to become, we must go back to the beginning. We must inspect the intentions and the creative genius of our Maker. We need to listen to God's opinion of the feminine gender before we are scathed by other people's unfair expectations, compared to ridiculous role models, and wounded by hurtful rejection. We have to discover what His assessment was of us at the exact moment in history that He created the very first woman.

⌒

"The fact that I am a woman does not make me a different kind of Christian, but the fact that I am a Christian does make me a different kind of woman."
—*Elisabeth Elliot,* Let Me Be a Woman

13

The "Muchness" of You

"God created man in His own image, in the image of God He created him; male and female He created them." —Genesis 1:27

After hearing a powerful truth, have you ever shouted these incredulous but fitting questions: *"What, are you kidding me? How did I miss this remarkable truth?"* The above potent Scripture, boldly stated in the very first chapter of the recorded Word of God, presents the fact that you, dear one, have been created in the very image of God! What could this possibly mean? How does this one piece of eternal knowledge impact your existence today?

It's true: you are like God. You were created to "look" like, act like, and talk like the God of the universe. You are His exact representation on planet earth in these early days of the twenty-first century. God has never created, nor will He ever create, second-rate, cheap imitations. He made you to be His consummate masterpiece. Now, of course, you are not God Himself; you are not deity. However, He made you to be just like Him in every way imaginable! God created both male and female in His very own image. You, my female friend, have the DNA of God inside of you! Aren't you absolutely overwhelmed by the fact that there is something in you that corresponds to something in the nature of God?

I know that we could never possibly know what exactly happened during this moment of creation. However, there is a still, small voice in me that has caused me to imagine it in this way: God needed a model to paint the picture of your life that would become His once-in-forever masterpiece. And so, our heavenly Father called His Son Jesus to sit down as His model. As the Creator extraordinaire studied the person of Jesus, He began to create you in His exact likeness. You are the duplicate of Jesus Christ on the earth today! Now, remember, you are not Jesus, but you were created to be just like Him! (See, for example, Ephesians 2:10.) How breathtaking is that!

This extraordinary bit of scriptural fact has the capacity to revolutionize your life and to re-arrange your internal value system. You weren't created to be a reflection of past rejection, childhood abuse, marital mistreatment, or emotional panic—you were created to reflect the character and nature of the God who is Love incarnate. You have been given the remarkable opportunity to be the hands, feet, and heart of Jesus to a world in pain.

The enemy of your soul, Satan, doesn't want you to tap into the richness of who you were created to be, and so he endeavors to distract you with distorted thinking, a misguided mind-set, and an illegitimate self-image. Knowing that you have been appointed to bring the light of Christ to the earth, his goal is to keep the world in darkness. Satan tries to abort your identity by convincing you that you are not enough and that you will never be enough—and absolutely nothing could be further from God's eternal and exciting truth!

A Woman of Blessing

At creation, after God completed His final masterpiece, humanity, in His own image, His next action was so wondrous that it never ceases to bring me to my knees in worship. He didn't walk away from His man and His woman, assuming that since He had created them, they could now exist separate from Him. He didn't give them a fatherly pat on the shoulder, flash them one final grin, and kick His heels in the air, as if His job was finally over.

This is what God the Father chose to do over the man and woman who were His finest work:

God blessed them; and God said to them, "Be fruitful and multiply, and fill the earth, and subdue it; and rule over the fish of the sea and over the birds of the sky and over every living thing that moves on the earth."   —Genesis 1:28

Don't miss it! Don't miss what God willfully did after He made man and woman in His image. He blessed them! God, the powerful and almighty Lord of the universe, performed an act of grace and dedication so rich and so rare that it reverberates through history to this very day. You, my friend, were not only made to be like God, but you have also been blessed by the God who made you!

The word *"blessed"* in this particular verse is the beautiful Hebrew word *barak*. The meaning of this term does not simply express a verbal blessing; it always includes a physical action as well. Generally, the physical action that would accompany the verbal blessing would be to bow, to kneel, or to salute. Oftentimes, it included all three of these actions.

Can you even begin to imagine that moment at the beginning of the history of the world? After God completed His magnum opus, the creation of man and woman, He likely then bowed His knee at those whom He had made. God was not worshipping the creation in that moment, but He was giving them His greatest gift—His personal and fatherly blessing. He was saluting those whom He had made. As Adam and Eve represent all of humanity, God was also saluting you.

Then, God not only made Adam and Eve in His image, but at this holy moment, He also gave them the honor of bequeathing them everything that He had previously created. He was declaring to Adam and to Eve, "All that I have created belongs to you! All that I am belongs now to you!"

Adam and Eve were the forerunners of all the generations that were yet to come. God spoke a blessing over them that echoes throughout the ages and comes to rest upon your life today.

A Woman of Authority

After God created man and woman, as you now know, He blessed this man and this woman. And then, after He blessed them, He gave them authority over all that He had created! He left them in charge of creation. How incredible is that?

You, my friend, have been left in charge in this world by the One who holds all authority and power!

Then God said, "…and to every beast of the earth and to every bird of the sky and to every thing that moves on the earth which has life, I have given every green plant for food"; and it was so. God saw all that He had made, and behold, it was very good. And there was evening and there was morning, the sixth day.

—Genesis 1:29–31

Even before God made man and woman in His own image, He planned to place them in a position of authority over His creation. Before He created what they looked like, before they realized their own potential, and even before they sniffed the fresh, fragrant air of Eden, God had a plan of power and authority for Adam and for Eve:

Then God said, "Let Us make man in Our image, according to Our likeness; and let them rule over the fish of the sea and over the

birds of the sky and over the cattle and over all the earth, and over
every creeping thing that creeps on the earth." —Genesis 1:26

God's eternal plan was set in motion when He created, when He blessed, and when He gave authority to the man and woman who were His finest work. You are not the "low woman on the totem pole," but you are the CEO, the CFO, and the COO of everything that God has created! He believes in you, and He deeply desires that you would believe in yourself the way that He does.

The highest heavens belong to the LORD, but the earth he has given
to mankind. —Psalm 115:16 (NIV)

When God Speaks

There is a phrase that the Holy Spirit uses two times in Genesis 1:28–29. It is a remark that is easy to overlook when reviewing the events of creation in all of their grandeur and miraculous moments. May I just point out to you this significant but quiet phrase?

*...and **God said** to them....* —Genesis 1:28

*Then **God said**....* —Genesis 1:29

This phrase, which is often lost in the fast-moving events of Genesis 1, holds great importance for those of us who are struggling with identity issues. This powerful phrase needs to rise to the top of our theology and dominate our belief system. God spoke blessing, purpose, and authority to His creation—and you are a significant part of His creation today! I pray that the words that were spoken in the Garden of Eden will reverberate with power and strength into the caverns of your heart this very day.

Whenever the phrase "God said" is used in Scripture, it is communicating more than just a verbal command. "God said" means that it was in

His heart and in His eternal plans to declare what subsequently came out of His mouth. God's intent is found in His Word. His purpose and His plans are found in His Word. God's Word is the gateway to His heart.

As the most favored of God's entire creation, you have been ordained by your Creator to rule and reign during your time on planet earth. It is God's perfect will and highest plan for you to be like Him, to be blessed by Him, and to be in charge of all that He created!

Every mineral, every tree, every animal, every flower, every wonder of this remarkable world has been placed here for you to cultivate and to delight in! He must think very highly of you!

Good! Good!

In Genesis, we see that God expressed an opinion about the world He had made. We can discover that opinion by reading the response that He had to everything He created:

---

*God saw that **the light was good**.*   —Genesis 1:4

*God called the dry land earth, and the gathering of the waters He called seas; and God saw that **it was good**.*   —Genesis 1:10

*The earth brought forth vegetation, plants yielding seed after their kind, and trees bearing fruit with seed in them, after their kind; and God saw that **it was good**.*   —Genesis 1:12

*God placed them [the sun, moon, and stars] in the expanse of the heavens to give light on the earth, and to govern the day and the night, and to separate the light from the darkness; and God saw that **it was good**.*   —Genesis 1:17–18

*God created the great sea monsters and every living creature that moves, with which the waters swarmed after their kind, and every winged bird after its kind; and God saw that **it was good**.*

—Genesis 1:21

*God made the beasts of the earth after their kind, and the cattle after their kind, and everything that creeps on the ground after its kind; and God saw that **it was good**.* —Genesis 1:25

The Holy Spirit, who empowered Moses to write this first book in the greatest Book that has ever been written, vividly describes God's reaction to all that He had made: He was pleased. As God stood on the precipice of history and stopped to look at all that had been fashioned by the word of His power (see, for example, Psalm 33:6), He knew that He had created a world of value, excellence, and happiness.

However, when God looked at the man and the woman that He had created, He had a higher opinion of their worth and value:

*God saw all that He had made, and behold, **it was very good**. And there was evening and there was morning, the sixth day.*

—Genesis 1:31

Only after fashioning man and woman in His very own image did God have the enthusiasm to declare, "Now, this is *very good!*"

Everything else that God had created was only "good" in His esteemed opinion. Giraffes were good and orchids were good; stars were good and gold was good. No matter how high the price of gold rises—you are worth infinitely more in God's value system. The Seven Wonders of the World are only "good" according to God, but you, who were made in His exact image, are very good, indeed!

You, whom God salutes and blesses, are very good in His unarguable opinion. You, who have been given authority to rule and reign, have been decreed as very good according to the wisest voice in eternity! You, who can use everything on this earth for your pleasure and benefit, are the consummate definition of the phrase "very good"!

In the ancient Hebrew language, there was no grammatical phrase that could express the adverb *very*. A single word in the Hebrew tongue did not exist that had the capacity to add emphasis to an adjective such as *good*. The way "very" was expressed in the Hebrew tongue was to use the chosen adjective not once, but twice. Therefore, what the pen of Moses wrote, under the inspiration of the Holy Spirit, was that you, as the crowning achievement of God's creation, are not merely good, but "good, good"!

In such languages as require it, this grammatical construction is sometimes known as "emphatic doubling." You are so good that God had to say it twice! The correct translation of the emphatic doubling in this verse is "exceedingly," "greatly," and "muchness." Isn't that a wonderful thought? You are the "muchness" of God's creation!

Act like It!

As stated earlier, our actions tend to be directed by our belief system. This truth is emphasized in Proverbs 23:7: "As [a person] *thinks within himself, so he is.*"

I want you to realize the importance of examining your belief system concerning your view of yourself, because you will never be able to live beyond who you think that you are. You will not break out of your own limitations until you first break into who God says that you are. So, now that you know, through His Word, who He says you are, are you ready to begin to act like it? Are you ready to respond in every situation like a woman of blessing and authority? Are you prepared to live a life that brings pleasure and delight to the heart of God?

If you can believe in your heart that God's Word is always true and that what He has declared always embodies His well-thought-out plans, then you must, you simply must, begin to think about yourself the way that

He does. When you submit your mind to the Word and the purpose of your Creator, it will impact the words you speak, the decisions you make, and the company you keep. Just for today, I want you to think about all that you are instead of all that you are not.

⌣͡

"We didn't get to choose our DNA, body type, birthday, time slot in history or many of our circumstances and challenges. But make no mistake, we do get to choose what kind of women we're going to be."
—Beth Moore

14

More to Your Story

The fact that God thinks you are "good, good" should absolutely change every detail of your life! You can wake up each morning with a spring in your step and a sparkle in your eyes as you partner with the God of the universe in being His representative on planet earth. Your job is to enjoy what He has created and to walk in your God-given and ordained authority. You should not complete one day of your life without acknowledging the unchangeable fact that you have been blessed by God.

But there is more to the story than that. And, as you and I both know, we do not always hear the birds singing, smell the aroma of fragrant flowers, or splash in liquid pools of joy. Some days are simply harder than others—just ask Eve.

Everything and Always and Never

God had given Adam and Eve authority over every living creature. He had also commanded them to enjoy every plant and every tree in their environment. He had not created the gorgeous Garden of Eden for His own pleasure, but rather for theirs. Eden was also the place where God intended to have a relationship with the crowning achievement of His creation. He wanted to walk with them and commune with them in this place of extraordinary beauty and divine atmosphere. I wonder if God had imagined the songs that they would sing together, the questions that Adam and Eve would ask, and the tender times of fellowship that they, and all the generations to come, would enjoy there.

God is a splendid communicator, and He was extremely thorough in His attempt to convey His intended strategy for life in the Garden of Eden to Adam and Eve. He didn't keep secrets from them but was careful to express His expectations:

Out of the ground the LORD *God caused to grow every tree that is pleasing to the sight and good for food; the tree of life also in the midst of the garden, and the tree of the knowledge of good and evil.... Then the* LORD *God took the man and put him into the garden of Eden to cultivate it and keep it. The* LORD *God commanded the man, saying, "From any tree of the garden you may eat freely; but from the tree of the knowledge of good and evil you shall not eat, for in the day that you eat from it you will surely die."*

—Genesis 2:9, 15–17

God was very explicit and exact in the instructions He gave to the man. He told Adam that everything was his—except for one thing. God prohibited Adam, and by extension, Eve, from eating of the tree of knowledge of good and evil. He said to those whom He had created, blessed, and loved, "Hey, listen! Trust Me on this! The tree of the knowledge of good and evil is not for you. Everything else belongs to you, and you can freely eat of it—you can have as much as you want of everything else. But, please, I am telling you that you don't need the tree of the knowledge of good and evil, and you actually don't want it. Everything else is yours!"

How will Adam and Eve respond to this specific instruction from God the Father? That's probably a foolish, rhetorical question, since we know how they responded to this very clear direction. However, I wanted to ask the question in the future tense because, for you, a more important question follows that one: How will *you* respond to the words and commands of God the Father?

When God speaks, the ones who have been blessed by God should listen and obey. When He instructs, the created should submit to the Creator. When He gives divine strategy, those under His authority should always defer to His wisdom. Always.

When you know who you are in the eyes of the Father, and when you agree with His assessment of your identity, then obedience is the expected response. Who wouldn't want to obey the One who made them and knows them best? Who wouldn't want to submit to the authority of the One who deems them as "good, good" and as the showpiece of His entire creation? When you extract your identity from the Father's opinion, obedience should never be a problem. Never.

Two Trees

Two trees are referenced in God's command to Adam: the first is *"the tree of life"* and the second is *"the tree of the knowledge of good and evil."* God told Adam and Eve that there was a definitive difference between the two trees. This was not a random command. There was a God-determined reason why Adam and Eve had access to one tree and not the other. And, in order for you to fully comprehend your true identity, you must understand the difference between these two famous trees.

The Tree of Life represents an intimate relationship with God and the amazing opportunity that we have to live out His kingdom on planet earth. God gave us a choice to love Him or not; God gave us a choice to obey Him or not. If He had not given us a choice, the Garden of Eden and our relationship with Him would have been a prison and not sweet communion. If we had been forced into a relationship with the Father, it would have been slavery and not freedom; it would have been a lifetime sentence and not eternal joy. In offering to Adam and Eve the Tree of Life, God was giving them the freedom to love Him and to choose Him over everything and everyone else.

God loves human beings completely and wants an intimacy with them that defies all limitations. Yet, as His created and blessed beings, we must choose Him. God has already chosen us, but He never forces Himself upon anyone. What was true for Adam and Eve is also true for you and me—we must *choose* Him.

The fruit on the Tree of Life is love, hope, joy, and kindness. An ordinary man or common woman can deliciously experience the manifestation of God when they partake of a relationship with Him. They discover the glorious fruit on the branches of the Tree of Life by accessing the promises of God and experiencing His power when they are weak. The Tree of Life symbolizes responding to God with humility and servanthood.

On the other hand, the Tree of Knowledge of Good and Evil is symbolic of what the culture of this world has to offer us. It represents what the world deems as valuable and acceptable. It is figurative of climbing the ladder of success and stepping on others all the way up. The Tree of Knowledge of Good and Evil epitomizes such responses as spewing your angry emotions over everyone in your pathway or believing that the political system has the final answer on everything. It buys into the world's view on sex, money, and entertainment.

Quite simply, the Tree of Life produces the culture of the kingdom of heaven, while the Tree of Knowledge of Good and Evil produces the culture of the enemy. The Tree of Knowledge of Good and Evil is not for you!

It was God's deepest desire for the crown of His creation to choose the ways of His kingdom, which includes intimacy with Him as well as extracting our opinion of ourselves from His opinion of us. He freely gave us fruit from the Tree of Life, which will always guarantee a life of blessing and abundance.

Even now, as I write these words, it's hard for me to imagine why anyone would choose death over life! It's absurd that I would ever agree with the culture of this world and disagree with God. It's ridiculous to think that I would prefer insecurity over divine identity.

A Rotten Deal

Have you heard of the TV game show *Let's Make a Deal?* It was popular in the 1960s and 1970s and has made a comeback in the last ten years. In case you don't remember it or haven't seen it in, let me explain the format to you as I remember it from years ago.

The audience always arrived dressed in ridiculous costumes like hot dogs or baseball bats or dinosaurs. The game show host would then choose the most absurdly dressed people among the audience members to be contestants. The host had a great sense of humor, and he would engage these willing participants in a guessing game or an activity that would end with either a great prize or a wacky reward. Oftentimes, a bizarrely dressed contestant would have to choose between "door number one," "door number two," and "door number three." Behind each of these doors were items that were either extremely valuable or extremely ludicrous. The entire audience would be engaged as they shouted to the players which door to choose.

My friend, you, too, have been given an option, but here it is between only two doors. Behind the first door grows the Tree of Life, with enormous benefits to be experienced both in this life and in eternity. The Tree of Life offers you victory and miracles; it presents joy and hope. However, behind door number two grows the garish Tree of Knowledge of Good and Evil. This door may guarantee temporary popularity, momentary success, and brief importance, but it will *never* fulfill you the way the Tree of Life will!

Which Will You Choose?

Can you hear it? Can you hear the angels and the saints of the ages cheering for you to choose the Tree of Life? Can you hear their encouragement for you to live a life of hope, joy, and abundance?

On the other side, can you hear the enemy and his nasty band of little wimps cajoling you and trying to deceive you into choosing the Tree of

Knowledge of Good and Evil? They don't want what's best for you—they want what is worst for you. They don't want you to know that you have been made in the image of God and that He has blessed you and given you authority. They want to make you a deal that you think you can't refuse—but you can!

Which tree will you choose? You have the advantage of knowing exactly what is behind each door. However, if you don't agree with God's assessment of who you were created to be, you will cave in to the culture and falsely believe that your only chance of fulfillment is in eating from the Tree of Knowledge of Good and Evil. But if you stand firm in agreement with God regarding who He created you to be, and choose the Tree of Life, it will add unmatched dignity and eternal significance to your life.

⌒

"We are not always going to feel like following God on the path to becoming the women He has asked us to be, which is why our choice has to be based on faith not feelings."
—*Sally Clarkson*

15

No Shame

If your assessment of yourself is in constant conflict with God's opinion of who you are, you will be confronted by perpetual shame. "Shame" might be defined as the painful feeling that often arises from the consciousness of being or doing something dishonorable or improper. When you refuse to see yourself the way that God sees you, you will go through life looking at yourself through the distorted lens of either pride or humiliation. You will often be ashamed of who you have become because you never really knew who you were created to be in the first place. If you don't agree with God concerning who He created you to be, you will never know the complete joy of living in the peace and confidence that only He can give.

But when you choose to live in communion with your Creator and to feast on the harvest that is offered from the Tree of Life, you will never need to know the meaning of the word "shame." Shame will not be part of your emotional constitution, nor even of your vocabulary. Even if you sometimes choose to sin or make a grievous mistake, the shame will be removed from you because you will be in communion with God. The secret to living a shame-free life is to eat the magnificent fruit from God's Tree of Life and to refuse the rotten fruit that grows from the Tree of Knowledge of Good and Evil.

True Identity

Let's continue our walk in the Garden of Eden with the first man and first woman that God ever created. We will eavesdrop on their conversations and observe their lifestyle. In doing so, I believe that we just might see ourselves in a historic and premiere moment.

And the man and his wife were both naked and were not ashamed.   —Genesis 2:25

This is a beautiful Scripture that is filled with the wonder of choosing well. It identifies what happens when men and women choose to eat only from the Tree of Life. This verse is the grand exhibit of the resulting confidence that accompanies agreeing with God concerning your identity.

Adam and Eve were not ashamed of their natural state because they looked at themselves in the same manner that God did. They were secure because they knew the One after whom they had been fashioned. I believe that they had the innate knowledge that the emphasis of life was not on their appearance but on what was within them. Adam and Eve had the DNA of God inside them—and so do you! Because they were so certain of His pleasure at their existence, they were walking in the authority, blessing, and delight that only intimacy with God can produce.

As human beings, we were always meant to extract our self-esteem from what has been placed within us by the God of the universe, and not from our outer packaging. The fact that the first man and woman had nothing to cover them was not bothersome to them at all. They knew their true identity and had no need at all to hide it. Adam and Eve were not ashamed, because they were filling themselves up with the presence of the One who had engineered their very existence! They were eating from the

Tree of Life and walking with God in the Garden of Eden in the cool of the day. There was no shame in that!

I hope that you will allow this powerful truth to seep down into the depth of your soul. When you choose the Tree of Life over the Tree of Knowledge of Good and Evil, you, too, will have absolutely no reason for shame. When you choose intimacy with Christ over the companionship of the world, you will walk in the power of His authority.

Don't Believe the Lie!

Has anyone ever lied to you? Has anyone ever tried to convince you of an untruth? There is great pain in realizing that someone does not respect you or love you enough to simply speak truth to you. Not only can being the recipient of a well-structured lie destroy your relationship with someone, but it can also do great damage to your self-esteem.

Our four-year-old granddaughter is a little piece of spice and sweetness all rolled into one miniature person. She is the youngest of four energetic and brilliant home-schooled children, and believe me, she doesn't get lost in the crowd! Her name is Elizabeth Joy, and we all affectionately call her "E.J."

E.J. is just learning how to write, and like most children, the first word that she wanted to write was her name. Her eleven-year-old sister, Olivia, patiently taught her how to write the letters *E* and *J*, and now she writes them on everything. She writes "E.J." with chalk on the sidewalk in front of her house, she writes "E.J." with a pencil on the back of the church bulletin, and she writes "E.J." on practically every piece of paper she can find in her home.

Having a room specifically set aside for teaching her children had long been a dream of my daughter-in-law Emily. She was finally able to move the daily homeschooling from the kitchen table to a room used exclusively for their classroom. She decorated this room with warmth and beauty, and we all love hanging out around the schoolroom table. Underneath this large, antique table is a white and light gray rug that keeps little feet from touching the cold floor below.

One day, not long ago, Emily walked into the schoolroom and noticed some markings on the formerly pristine carpet beneath the table. Written there in red marker were two solitary letters. You guessed it—*E* and *J*.

When Emily confronted this creative piece of feminine potential about the letters on the rug, Elizabeth Joy insisted that she had not done it. Her mother gave her several opportunities to confess and tell the truth, but she refused to give in. After tears and discipline, E.J. finally told the truth. Yes—she had done it. She was merely trying to practice her name in the schoolroom like the other children did. (Of course, they all practice their penmanship in books that are designed for such an exercise, not on the schoolroom rug!)

When the atmosphere had calmed down a bit and Emily was snuggling with E.J. on the family couch, Emily asked her why she had lied. E.J. looked up at her mom with snapping blue eyes and confessed, "Because I wanted you to believe me."

Isn't that the reason why anyone lies? Specifically, a liar lies because he or she deeply desires for the listener to believe the lie.

An Atomic Lie

We are about to listen in on the most explosive lie that has ever been told in all of recorded history. We are about to gasp in horror over the epic damage that ensued. The reason that this gargantuan lie was uttered by the conceiver of every other falsehood that would be told in the millennia to follow was because he was intent on getting the listener to believe him. The question that was relevant then is still relevant for each of us today: Will you believe what Satan the deceiver says, or will you believe what the Father says?

Now the serpent was more crafty than any beast of the field which the LORD *God had made. And he said to the woman, "Indeed, has God said, 'You shall not eat from any tree of the garden'?" The woman said to the serpent, "From the fruit of the trees of the garden we may eat; but from the fruit of the tree which is in the middle of the garden, God has said, 'You shall not eat from it or touch it, or you will die.'" The serpent said to the woman, "You surely will not die! For God knows that in the day you eat from it your eyes will be opened, and you will be like God, knowing good and evil."* —Genesis 3:1–5

Eve believed the lie that was spoken by the one whom Scripture identifies as *"the father of lies"* (John 8:44). Poor self-esteem and shame always begin by believing the deception that is spoken by the enemy of the people of God. He is infamous for his lies and knows of no other way to communicate. The only words that come out of his decrepit little mouth are falsehoods, distortions, fabrications, and fallacies.

"You're too fat!"

"You're not intelligent enough!"

"No one will ever marry you!"

"You are poor because God doesn't love you!"

"You are sick because God is punishing you!"

If you are not absolutely certain of how the Father sees you, you will create the volatile risk of believing the lies of the enemy. The only way you can be assured of God's confidence in you is by eating from the Tree of Life and staying in intimate communion with Him. When you choose to obey Him in these matters, you will know that you know that you know who you are and, perhaps more importantly, who you are not.

An Ignored Truth

Let's reread two verses from this section of Scripture so that I can point out to you an amazing piece of truth that Eve ignored.

*The serpent said to the woman, "You surely will not die! For God knows that in the day you eat from it your eyes will be opened, **and you will be like God**, knowing good and evil."* —Genesis 3:4–5

I believe in writing notations in my Bible. Do you? I often take notes from anointed sermons and write them in the margins. I also feel free to underline words or verses that stand out to me during my daily quiet time. And I often make personal notes over and around verses when the Holy Spirit speaks to me as I am communing with my Creator.

One January morning, as I was studying the beginning chapters of Genesis, the Holy Spirit showed me a truth so significant and moving that I began to cry. This wasn't a pretty cry that cold, winter morning. I didn't have tears sweetly falling down my cheeks as I gently wiped them away before my mascara began to run. No—it was a gut-heaving, shoulder-shaking, nose-blowing cry that came over me that day. Do you want to know why?

Eve was already like God! She didn't need to believe the lie or eat the fruit to be like God because she had already been made in the exact image of her Creator! Now, in my well-worn Bible, I have written beside this verse in dark black ink, "Eve was already like God, and so are you, Carol! So are you!"

It amazes me that this woman, who knew the true blessing and wonder of relationship with God, believed the lie of the enemy. It astounds me that Eve, who was filling her life with sweet communion with the Father, ignored the truth and even considered the deception. She chose to believe the lie of the enemy, and I have often done the same.

As women of God in the twenty-first century, we have a choice: we either believe what God has said in His Word, or we believe the lies of Satan. We either believe that God loves us and blesses us, or we believe the lies of the enemy. We either believe that we were made in the image of God for His glorious purposes, or we believe the lies of the enemy.

The choice between believing the eternal, powerful Word of God or believing the weak lies of the enemy is where that infamous fork in the road of self-esteem occurs. If you don't believe who God says you are, you will be beguiled by the perjury that is presented to you by Satan.

I have often wondered what would have happened at this point in Eve's story if she had told Satan to shut up! I have imagined what outcome would have taken place if she had told the serpent to take a hike back to hell. I have pondered the story that history would have written if Eve had stomped on the head of the serpent and walked away. We will never know the answer to these musings, but we can discover what will happen when ordinary women—like you and me—tell the enemy to shut up! We can see a miraculous and different outcome when we determine that we will believe the truth of the Father rather than the lies of the enemy. We can live an entirely different life due to the simple fact that we determine to believe that we are, indeed, who God says that we are!

The impact of this one central truth cannot be overstated: If you refuse the identity that God has lavishly given to you, you will find that the ensuing choices you make in life will not strengthen you as a woman, but rather weaken you. They will not set you in your destiny but instead send you on a path to destruction. It all begins with the choice whether to believe the Word of God.

When you hear statements made or questions posed, ask yourself, "Who said it?" And then coach yourself with the following piece of revolutionary truth: *"If God didn't say it…then I don't believe it!"*

⌒

"That's the key: not believing the lies, fixing our eyes on Jesus
and walking in that truth."
—*Joanna Gaines*

16

Who Told You?

I consider myself a fairly interesting person whose interests and preferences are expansive and eclectic. I am a Christmas-aholic, yet I despise cold weather and snow. I love long days spent at the beach with my toes in the sand and a great book in my hands while the sun is beating down upon me. Unlike many women, I hate to shop, but I love college basketball! And some of my best friends are people under ten years old.

However, the one very boring aspect of my life is my taste in movies. I call myself a "movie elitist" because there are so few movies that capture my attention. I don't want one word of profanity in a movie, absolutely no sex scenes (although I do love romance), and certainly not one drop of blood or guts on the screen! As you can imagine, this is very limiting when it comes to choosing a movie that I can watch with my husband, other family members, or friends. What often happens in my home is that we revert back to the same ten to fifteen movies that we have watched countless times before, simply because my movie guidelines leave little room for exploration.

When my husband and I sit down to watch a Carol-approved movie that we have seen tens of times already, we can almost quote the dialogue verbatim, and we find ourselves talking back to the characters. We want to save them from the painful circumstances they are going to create or the mistakes they are going to make.

My husband has a sparkle in his eye as he says to me, "Oh no, Carol! He is going to do it again! He is going to (rob that bank...or leave his wife... or drop out of school)."

I feel much the same way when I read the story of Eve. Although I have read it probably hundreds of times, each time I want to cry out, "No, Eve! Don't do it! Don't eat the fruit! Don't believe the lie!"

She Does It Again

When the woman saw that the tree was good for food, and that it was a delight to the eyes, and that the tree was desirable to make one wise, she took from its fruit and ate; and she gave also to her husband with her, and he ate. —Genesis 3:6

The history of the people of God pivots on this one verse. This is the singular biblical event that changed all of life's possibilities for you and for me. When Eve spent time in conversation with the serpent, listened to his lies, and then believed them, it was a moment of colossal implications. Let's break this verse down phrase by horrible phrase and allow this massive mistake to grip us—one thought and one choice at a time.

When the woman saw that the tree was good for food....

Eve was captivated by a temporary fix; she wanted food more than she wanted fellowship with God. What is it that you and I want more than intimacy with Christ? Sex? Spending? Eating? Anger? Bitterness? The enemy can only tempt us with something that is temporary—and he has become an expert at it.

...and that it was a delight to the eyes....

My, my, my! From the beginning of time, Satan knew what would tempt women, didn't he? He knew that we love beautiful things, attractive settings, and lovely accessories. He didn't choose something ugly with which to tempt our sister Eve, but he used something beautiful. However, like Eve, what I have discovered in my life is that the beauty that he tempts me with is temporary—and it quickly becomes ugly.

The devil lives in darkness, and he is a liar. But because of the price that Jesus paid on the cross, he has absolutely no power. What he does possess is the ability to twist the truth just enough to make it seem believable. He is conniving and chooses something that will entice us, not repel us.

...and that the tree was desirable to make one wise...

Once again, the serpent taunted Eve with an unfair exchange. In this moment, Eve obviously wasn't thinking about what God had already said about her. She falsely believed that she wouldn't be all that she was capable of becoming without eating this piece of forbidden fruit. Poor Eve.

The Hebrew word translated *"wise"* in the phrase *"to make one wise"* is not the same word that is generally used to describe the wisdom of God. The word that is most often used to describe divine wisdom is *chokmah*, which is a powerful term that implies wisdom of every kind. It is not limited to situations or to learned knowledge, but it is an authoritative and all-knowing wisdom. However, the word that the Holy Spirit uses to describe the type of wisdom that Eve desired is *sakal*. It signifies what we might call "common sense" or even "street smarts." This is the type of wisdom that is obtained from a life experience or from an observation.

There is no earthly wisdom or knowledge that can ever compare to what the Lord has offered to us. We were fashioned to be just like Him and to even think His thoughts! How utterly amazing is that? Your value as a woman is based upon an eternal promise and principle, not on words of deceit or temporary solutions.

My heart is broken for Eve as I once again rewind this ancient scene in my mind. I still can't believe she was that foolish or shortsighted to be brainwashed by the devastating lies of the enemy. However, as I evaluate my own life decisions and replay conversations and choices that I have made, I realize that I am like Eve in many, many ways. Often, I default to pleasure or the quick fix rather than the divine identity I have been given by my Father. I forget that I have His DNA living and active inside of me, and trade my dignity for a temporary delight.

If Eve had taken the time to remember what God had said to her, I believe that the outcome would have been decidedly different, don't you?

Eyes Wide Open and Naked

Then the eyes of both of them were opened, and they knew that they were naked; and they sewed fig leaves together and made themselves loin coverings. —Genesis 3:7

I hope that you read the shame and horror that is hidden among the words of this verse of Scripture. In an instant, Adam and Eve were astonished at what they had done, and they looked at each other with both dismay and utter shock. The choice that they had made based upon fiction rather than upon truth changed how they viewed themselves. No longer were they able to walk confidently in the identity that God had bestowed upon them, but they were ashamed. So great was their insecurity that they were forced to cover themselves.

It's ridiculous to picture Adam and Eve frantically searching around for something—for anything—to cover their private parts, isn't it? Can you imagine these two lovebirds scrounging around with sheer panic as they endeavored to discover a leaf or flower large enough to conceal what now brought them shame? And yet, I wonder, how ridiculous we, too, look to the Holy Spirit when we try to cover our shame with excuses, with spending, with eating, or with entertainment. How must the Father, who created us to be glorious, feel when we falsely believe that just one more drink or one more raise or one more academic degree will cover our shame?

The eyes of the first man and woman were opened to a worldly mind-set. No longer did they view the world through the purity of their God-ordained existence, but they began to see themselves as the devil did. They saw themselves as cheap bait for the enemy rather than valuable treasure in the kingdom of God. They had traded the truth for a lie, and now, although God had created them to live a blessed life, they would never see themselves as good enough. Now, while God viewed them as His highest masterpiece, they would approach life supposing that they were lacking in esteem and dignity.

How do you view yourself? Have you traded the truth for a lie, much like Adam and Eve did? Are you frantically searching for something new or different to add more value to your life? Be at peace, my friend, and reestablish your intimacy with Christ. It is in His presence that you will be reminded of who you really are. It is His voice that will assure you of your worth and your identity. Nothing else will do—simply nothing.

More Heartbreak

It was not uncommon for Adam and Eve to hear the voice of God calling their names in the garden. Prior to this interaction with the serpent, and their subsequent response to him, I can imagine that when God called, this first man and this first woman ran to the Father, even took hold of His hand, before they perhaps sat down together under some exotic tree. Maybe, as they ate from the gorgeous, dripping fruit, they discussed eternity, worship, and their ordained destiny. Such a scene from the life of Adam and Eve was now merely part of their memory book. It would never happen again.

They heard the sound of the LORD God walking in the garden in the cool of the day, and the man and his wife hid themselves from the presence of the LORD God among the trees of the garden.
—Genesis 3:8

I hope that you take the time to allow the heartbreak in this verse to saturate your very soul.

+ This time...because they had chosen poorly, they hid from God and from His purposes for their lives.

+ This time...because they had bought into the lie, they were unable to walk in their God-given identity.

+ This time...because they had not stood upon the word of God, they sacrificed His blessing and His presence.

+ This time...because the deceit of Satan convinced them that they were not enough, they ran *from* God rather *to* Him.

When we believe the lies of Satan that we are not enough and that identity and purpose is found in compromise, we, too, will hide from God. We will cover ourselves with thoughts that rationalize our behavior, we will spend ourselves into bankruptcy, we will compromise our bodies, we will eat until we are sick, and we will forget what the truth actually is.

Before we tackle one more verse in this descriptive biblical account, let me remind you what the truth is concerning your identity:

+ You have been made in the exact image-likeness of God.

+ You are blessed by the God who created you.

+ You have been given authority by the God who created you.

+ In the Creator's expert opinion, you are "good, good"!

Don't ever believe anything that contradicts what God has decreed concerning your identity and your purpose. You are enough, my friend. You are more than enough. When the day comes that the enemy tries to convince you that you are not enough, walk away and remind yourself who God created you to be. When the day comes that the enemy taunts you with His cheap lies, declare the Word of God over His shrill and scratchy voice. When the day comes that you must decide who you are in the deepest part of you, eat from the Tree of Life and be filled.

A Question That Deserves an Answer

Then the L ORD *God called to the man, and said to him, "Where*
are you?" —Genesis 3:9

The interesting thing about this verse is that God did, indeed, know
where Adam and Eve were. He knows where all of His children are every
minute of every day. We can run from God, but we can never hide from
Him. We serve a God who perpetually sees and knows us, and yet is constantly looking for us. God knew where His beloved children Adam and
Eve were, just as He knows where you are, and yet He deeply wanted them
to reveal themselves to Him. It is what the Father always wants—He
desires for His children to simply say, "Here I am, Dad! I'm right here!"

[Adam] said, "I heard the sound of You in the garden, and I was
afraid because I was naked; so I hid myself." And [God] said,
"Who told you that you were naked? Have you eaten from the tree
of which I commanded you not to eat?" —Genesis 3:10–11

Whenever a child of God decides to listen to the lies of the enemy, they
begin to go down a slippery slope. It starts with compromise, and then it
quickly proceeds to shame. Trying to cover yourself with outrageous and
ill-fitting reactions will affect your relationship with your Creator. First,
you will hide, and then you will fear His very presence. How did all that
happen? How did Adam and Eve progress from having an intimate, lively
relationship with their Creator to one of shame and fear? The avalanche
started the instant that Eve believed the lie.

God's first response to His son Adam was, *"Who told you that you were*
naked?"

Remember that God already knew what Adam and Eve had done; He
is omniscient and is always aware of what His children are doing. God
knew the truth, yet He desired for Adam to come to Him and tell Him the

truth. That is precisely what the Father wants from you, as well, even when you have believed the lie. He wants you to run into His presence and talk to Him about the choices you have made. He will not be surprised to hear them, for He already knows about them. He wants to hear your voice and to draw you back into relationship with Himself.

In Adam's case, God asked, *"Who told you that you were naked?"* Perhaps you have heard the Father asking you a very similar question:

"Who told you that you weren't good enough?"

"Who told you that you were too fat?"

"Who told you that you weren't smart?"

"Who told you that you were unlovable?"

"Who told you that you had no value?"

God knows the answer, and yet He asks, just the same. God knows the source of your insecurity and shame, and yet He draws you into conversation with Him. He knows why you are hiding and why you try to cover your true identity with temporary and foolish choices, yet He longs to hear your voice.

Who told Adam that he was naked? It is a question that still deserves an answer. It was quite simply the Tree of Knowledge of Good and Evil that had identified Adam as being naked. It was the world's system of value that had defined who Adam had become, because he and Eve had listened to the lies of the enemy.

You are the steward of your own self and of who God created you to be. Steward your identity and the days of your life well, my friend. Steward your life so that every minute of your days and every morsel of your identity brings glory to the One who created you.

⌒

"Satan is so much more in earnest than we are—he buys up the opportunity while we are wondering how much it will cost."
—*Amy Carmichael*

17

You Are More Than Enough

God is a genius at everything that He does, and He fully expressed His indescribable brilliance when He created you! Just as He designed the first man and woman, He created you with three distinct and separate parts. He created you with a body, a spirit, and a soul. Each of these amazing facets of our being is significant.

Don't Ignore This

Now, listen—I know women. At this point, I know that some of you are going to skip ahead or try to skim through this chapter. Don't do it! This is important stuff as you try to understand who you are, why you are, and all that you have the potential to become! I promise that I will try to make it as interesting and engaging as possible!

Your Packaging

Your body is only your packaging, my friend. Your body does not define you, and it does not determine your destiny or your value. The world might base its judgment of you upon your facial features and your body, but that's because it looks only at the outward appearance. The world doesn't see what God sees! Your body is only the frame that holds the masterpiece that the Creator made. Please don't go through life disappointed by how you look or by the type of packaging you are in.

"Beauty is only skin deep" were the wise words of my grandmother, quoting the famous adage, and I have tried to remind myself often of their intrinsic truth. Some of the most beautiful women I know would not be considered attractive on Broadway or in Hollywood; their beauty shines from deep within them, and they are breathtaking, indeed! Conversely, some of the women whose faces might appear in *People* or *Vogue* magazine don't have a beautiful bone in their bodies due to their lack of human kindness and the way they treat other people. Your packaging is temporary and does not tell the whole story of your life.

Your Spiritual DNA

Your spirit is the part of you that reflects the DNA of God, and it is where His blessing is imparted to your extraordinary life. Your spirit is the aspect of you that hears the voice of God and responds willingly to Him. Your spirit is the component of your makeup where the kingdom of God is established, where the fruits of the Spirit are cultivated, and where you walk by faith and not by sight. Your spirit should be the most powerful part of your makeup as you travel through life. It is infinitely more important to cultivate a beautiful spirit than it is to develop a lovely outward appearance. Your spirit enables you to walk in your destiny and not in a compromised, second-rate future.

Your Ability to Choose

The third part of your God-engineered makeup is your soul, which is comprised of your mind, will, and emotions. Your soul is empty until you fill it with something. From the beginning of time, in the Garden of Eden, it was always God's plan that you would fill up your soul with Him! It was always the high call of God that you, as His precious child, would take your soul to eat at the luscious Tree of Life. It was always His intention that you, who have been made in His divine image, would choose intimacy with Him over intimacy with the world. It was also His heart's desire that you would fill up the hollow places in your soul with all that He has to offer.

True beauty radiates from a woman's soul. The sad news of our existence is that we have filled up our souls with the values of a culture whose priority is not God and His Word, and we have believed the outrageous lie that God isn't enough. We have turned to clothes, men, bank balances, entertainment, and addictions to fill up the empty places in our hearts. Those things are like the contorted mirrors we view ourselves in at the House of Mirrors at a fair. You will never understand how God sees you, see the real you, or become the genuine you if you foolishly try to fill your soul with trash rather than with treasure.

As women of the twenty-first century, we have allowed bathroom scales, TV shows that lack morality, and vulgar music lyrics to fill the caverns of our minds and emotions. If that is what you feast on throughout the course of your life, everything about who you were created to be will be warped out of proportion. Do not gaze at the culture and believe that it is your compass to success or wholeness. The world in which you live should be looking at you as their compass to abundant and extraordinary living because you have a soul that is vibrant and powerful!

God gave you a soul so that you would choose Him. God gave you a soul so that you would be a woman who walks in divine destiny and confident identity. God gave you a soul so that you could lavishly spread joy, hope, peace, and righteousness in your world. God gave you a soul that flourishes only when you spend time with Him. Your loveliness was never meant to be defined by your outward appearance; your true beauty was always meant to be a reflection of your relationship with your Father.

So, who do you think you are? Will you agree with God and eat from the Tree of Life? Or, will you enter into a conversation with the enemy, listen to his weak lies, and have the audacity to believe them? You choose, my friend, you choose.

You can choose to believe what the enemy says about you or what the Bible says about you. You can listen to Satan or you can tell him to shut up! You can fill your soul with the things of the world that will never satisfy, or you can fill your soul with the wonderful presence of the Father. I can't choose for you—only you can choose for yourself. It is your choice.

Stolen Identity

There was an ordinary man by the name of Wes Thompson who had the wretched experience of having had his identity stolen from him for thirty-five years of his life. The trigger event that caused Wes to lose his identity happened at a college party in 1974. Wes's brother, while he was drunk, gave away key factors about Wes's life. He told a conniving stranger where and when Wes was born, and his mother's maiden name. Wes's brother also gave this infidel other identifying factors that would eventually be used against him.

The derelict man who stole Wes's identity was eventually able to get his Social Security number and secure car loans in his name. This imposter incurred $139,000 in debt under Wes's name in one year alone. He declared bankruptcy in Wes's name, earned a driver's license in his name, and applied for health benefits in his name.

As you can imagine, the frustration that Wes experienced was exhausting and unrelenting. Too many times to count, he was denied loans because the imposter had ruined his credit. When the man who stole Wes's identity was finally discovered after thirty-five long years, Wes joyfully declared, "I was at the end of my rope! Now I am on top of the world—it's like I have been released from prison!"

Make no mistake about it—someone has stolen your identity, too, and his name is Satan. He is also known as the accuser of the people of God. (See Revelation 12:10.) His derelict self has not only stolen your identity, but he has also absconded with your purpose, your productivity, and your health. How did this happen? There was a trigger event that caused your identity to be stolen, just as there was for Wes.

The instant that you doubted God's Word and His love for you was the trigger event that allowed the enemy to swoop in and take over. To regain your identity, you must believe that what God says is eternally true, not merely situationally appropriate. You must understand that while you were still in your mother's womb, whether or not she wanted you or had planned for you, God was so excited about the potential of your life that He was jumping up and down!

If you long to dream again and to hear God's voice concerning His plan for your life, you need to stop focusing on all that you are not and begin to gaze on who He created you to be. You must immediately stop agreeing with the devil's opinion of you and begin today to agree with God's assessment of your life! Your identity as a daughter of the King is as constant as constant gets.

The Bible has stated its case—it is your choice to believe it or not.

⌣

"Be who God meant you to be and you
will set the world on fire."
—*St. Catherine of Siena*

18

Your Name Is...

Over the years, my husband, Craig, and I have agreed on almost everything—spending habits, where to go on vacation, how to decorate our home, and in what manner to discipline our children. However, the one issue on which we have never been able to agree is what to name our children. I have loved perfectly wonderful and unique names like Sterling, Brighton, and Everleigh. He preferred the classic names of Emily, Sarah, and Rachel.

When I would bring up a potential name (an incredible one, let me add) such as Nora or Jillian, he would respond with a grimace as he rolled his handsome blue eyes and said something like, "Oh, Carol! There was a girl in the second grade whose name was Nora, and she was just awful!"

"But, Craig," I would instantly reply, "that was nearly thirty years ago, and you don't even know her anymore!"

Finally, the way we would always reach a truce when it came to choosing a name for one of our babies was by agreeing on the meaning of the name. We both believed that the meaning behind the baby's name was as important—often, even more important—as the look or sound of the name.

Through my years of mothering and hearing the names chosen by other young families to bequeath upon their children, what has amazed me are the cultural crazes in certain decades. In the early 1980s, one of the most popular names for a little boy was Jason. One of my friends was a kindergarten teacher, and she told me that one year in the mid-1980s, she had twelve boys in her classroom—and ten of them were named Jason!

And then there are the names that movie stars and entertainers choose for their children, among them Apple, Blanket, and Cosmo. Sometimes, names can be more of a curse than a blessing! There was a girl who went to my high school whose name was "Beverly Beverly"! Her first name was the same as her last name—who does that to a child?

The name of our firstborn son, Matthew, means "gift of God"—and what a gift he has been! We named our second son Christopher, which means "bearer of Christ." Chris has always taken the presence and Spirit of Christ everywhere he has gone. Jordan, our son who was born after we lost five babies, has this beautiful meaning to his name: "one who carries on." We have always believed that Jordan would be the one to carry on in ministry after us.

Then—after three boys—do you know what you name a girl? Why, you name her Joy, of course! Actually, you name her Carolyn Joy, which means "song or dance of joy." "Joy-Belle," as she is affectionately known, has always lived up to her name.

And then, when we experienced a surprise pregnancy when I was nearly forty years old, we decided to name this sweet little caboose after both of her grandmothers—Joni Rebecca. The meaning of Joni (also Joan) is "God is gracious," while the meaning of Rebecca is "to tie or to bind." We believe that God has tied His grace to the life of Joni and that He has bound Himself to her.

YOUR NAME IS... 157

Names are also of great importance to Father God, and He has chosen to give you specific names that carry extraordinary meanings. Now that you know that God has created you, blessed you, and given you His authority, let's look in the Word of God to discover some of the names that have been assigned to you. You are always on God's mind, and the meanings of your names were strategically chosen by Him to reveal His purpose and plan for your life. The meaning of a given name always reveals one's identity. If you were to look up these names in a Bible dictionary, you would jump for joy, knowing that God has strategically named you with purpose.

It is vital to take the time to find your identity in the Word of God, or you will be doing a great disservice to the world in which you live. If you sadly choose to copy someone else's identity, the world will never receive the gift that was meant to be you! You are uniquely "you," with all of your quirks, strengths, and weaknesses. However, the "you" that you were meant to be smacks of the family's genetic pool from which you came. So, let's begin!

Your Name Is Light

In any average family, there is generally some type of similarity among the siblings. I don't particularly look like my brother, but we do have the same contagious laugh that bursts forth and becomes nearly uncontrollable in inappropriate situations in life.

According to Scripture, Jesus is your older Brother (see, for example, Romans 8:29), and He describes Himself in this way: *"While I am in the world, I am the Light of the world"* (John 9:5). Jesus came to planet earth to bring heaven's eternal light to those of us who were living in darkness. From eternity, He knew that it was in His job description to shine God's light in a dark world.

The people who walk in darkness will see a great light; those who live in a dark land, the light will shine on them. —Isaiah 9:2

The night that Jesus was born on earth, the sky exploded with a grand display of lights and glory because the Light of the World had arrived in the form of a baby. And, it was a light, or a star, that led the wise men to the Christ child.

You were created to be like your Big Brother, Jesus, in too many ways to count! One of the most significant similarities that you share with Him is that both of you were called to bring light to the world at your moment in history. These are the words spoken by your elder Sibling, Jesus, to you:

You are the light of the world. A city set on a hill cannot be hidden; nor does anyone light a lamp and put it under a basket, but on the lampstand, and it gives light to all who are in the house. Let your light shine before men in such a way that they may see your good works, and glorify your Father who is in heaven.

—Matthew 5:14–16

The physical presence of Jesus is no longer on planet earth, and we have been designated to take His place because His Spirit lives within us. We have been given the powerful mantle of bringing light to the dark world in which we live. We are called to be candlesticks, light fixtures, street lamps, and flashlights through which His light shines. Our family is in the business of light-bringing, and now it is your turn to lead the family company!

I have often heard a particular descriptive phrase concerning one of my dear friends, Kelly. When people meet her, they often say, "Well, her smile just lights up the room!" Kelly has not led a particularly easy life, having been raised in a dysfunctional home from childhood and having watched her father die when she was a young girl. But this fact remains: Kelly's smile and presence light up every room that she enters. She is a spark of Christmas joy and a display of Fourth of July fireworks, all rolled into one dynamite package.

When you enter into a conversation with someone, the light of Christ should enter it. When you walk into a relationship, the brightness of God's presence should bring acceptance and healing. Your life was meant to be a celebration of light and an explosion of the presence of God! The persona that you embody should be lighting up your entire neighborhood! Your countenance should shine as bright as the stars as you bring Jesus into your home and into your workplace.

Unfortunately, many of us have suffered power outages caused by the storms in our lives. We have allowed unstable circumstances and fractious people to snuff out the light that was meant to shine brightly within. We have allowed bitterness, unforgiveness, worry, and doubt to pull the plug on our connection to the source of heaven's grand light displayed in our lives.

God's plan to name you "light" was strategic; it was not chosen blindly based upon some cultural craze. I believe that when you were delivered to planet earth, God was elated over the light that He had placed within you and therefore that you were going to bring to this darkened world during your moment in history. Perhaps God's plan was that you would dispel darkness in the realm of education or that your presence would be like fireworks in the political arena. Maybe the reason that He named you "light" was so that you would shine His lamp of goodness onto the darkened streets of the entertainment industry. Perhaps the Lord placed you in a dark and contentious office building to light it up like a sunny day on a tropical beach. God had such confidence in your particular brand of light that He knew nothing would be able to quench the light of Christ within you—neither disappointment, nor discouragement, nor rejection.

You are the light of the world!

You know, even as Christians, we don't like dark places and tend to avoid them. We try to stay as far away as we can from dingy relationships, gloomy workplaces, and dim environments, but the truth is that dark places need the light that only we can bring.

Often, women will say to me, "Carol, please pray that I can get a new job. My office is such a place of darkness and confusion. Pray that God will give me a job in the ministry."

"What!" I have been known to respond incredulously. "You *are* in the ministry! Perhaps God has placed you in a pitch-black work environment because He needs you to turn on a few light switches! I will not pray that you will get out of there, but I will pray that you will shine brighter and brighter!"

I believe that God needs His sparkplugs in messy and dark situations, not so that we are influenced by the dark but so that we dispel it with the light of Christ within us. Don't dread darkness and don't allow it to change your identity. You have been called to light up darkness. No amount of darkness is able to hide even a spark of light!

The same God who spoke the sun, moon, and stars into existence has declared that you, dear one, are the light of His world. You have been given more energy, light, kilowatts, heat, and amps than the sun, moon, and stars combined. The greatest Light in all of eternity now lives inside you. So… it is time for you to light up the world in which you live! Start living up to your given name! An immeasurable Light has been placed within you for a reason. You are the light of the world!

Your Name Is Salt

You are the salt of the earth; but if the salt has become tasteless, how can it be made salty again? It is no longer good for anything, except to be thrown out and trampled under foot by men.

—Matthew 5:13

At first thought, it might seem more exciting to be identified as "light" than "salt." You might suppose that the only benefit of salt is that it is very cheap to buy, and that its outstanding deficit is that it causes high blood pressure. However, if you have ever eaten a salt-free meal or been put on a salt-restricted diet, you readily know the wonderful compliment that comes with being identified as salt.

Salt makes food taste better, and you, by your very existence, should make the life of everyone around you taste a little bit better. Your joy, your habits, and your hope should be attractive to those around you. They should want what you have because you have an attractive spirit and your life just tastes so good to everyone who takes a bite!

When I was growing up, my Irish grandmother used to cook a savory roast beef for Sunday dinner. One day, I noticed that she pricked the meat with a fork in several places before she salted it and placed it in the oven. When I innocently asked her why she stuck the long prongs of the fork into the meat, she said, "Oh, child! That's because I want the goodness of the salt to go way down deep into the meat. We don't want only the top to be salted, but we want the salt to reach all the way through."

I have often thought about that long-ago conversation as I have contemplated what Jesus meant when He identified His family as *the salt of the earth.* I believe that just as it is necessary to have salt go into the deepest parts of the food it is flavoring, we, as believers, need to take the time to go deeply into people's lives. Rather than merely sprinkling our joy as we quickly pass through someone's life, we must take the time to ask questions, to listen, and to spend large amounts of time getting to know them. It is in investing time and energy in relationships that the salt of our lives will make a definite difference in theirs.

Salt not only brings out the amazing flavor of a nice piece of meat, a casserole dish, or a healthy vegetable, but it is also used as a tenderizing agent. When you salt a piece of tough meat and allow the salt to linger through every ounce of it, the result is a much more tender piece of meat to be enjoyed. When Jesus named Christians "salt," He was identifying us as a "tenderizing agent" in the world in which we live. Our presence in people's tough lives should soften them to experience the peace and sweetness of our Savior. Their lives should be less stiff and sinewy because we are in them. Our goal is to deliver a gentle way of looking at life that people might have been missing before.

How can your presence in the lives of those around you lighten their load and ease their way?

When you see a harried mother in the grocery store line, give her a word of encouragement. That is when you are acting as an agent of salt.

When you talk to the person who serves you in the drive-through line, use gentle words and be friendly. That is when you are acting as an agent of salt.

When you interact with your in-laws or elderly relatives, be kind and listen patiently. That is when you are acting as an agent of salt.

Another benefit of being a salty person is that salt is known as a preservative; it keeps things from becoming rotten. Your presence in someone else's life should preserve it from becoming sour and disgusting. Your perspective on the economy, on politics, on parenting, and on marriage should bring a sweet breath of refreshing air into a conversation. That is when you are acting as an agent of salt. You are living up to your name!

An additional use of salt that you might not have been aware of is that, in the ancient world, salt was used as a fertilizer. Farmers knew that if they sprinkled salt on the soil while the seeds were lying dormant that their crop would be greener and have a greater harvest. You are called by Jesus Himself to be a fertilizer in the world in which you live! Simply because you show up, situations and relationships should be more fertile and more productive. The world should be richer because you are in it. Just as fertilizers enable the soil to grow more produce, your influence should encourage the world to grow in devotion to Jesus Christ. *That* is when you are living up to your name.

You are salt!

〜

"Jesus came to announce to us that an identity based on
success, popularity and power is a false identity—an
illusion! Loudly and clearly he says: 'You are not what the
world makes you; but you are children of God.'"
—*Henri J. M. Nouwen*, Here and Now

19

You Are Who He Says You Are

Do you believe it yet? Have you decided that it is time to agree with the Father who purposefully and gloriously named you? Are you coming to the realization that you are exactly who God says that you are? Our Father is infinite in all of His ways, and I have discovered that He loves to attach eternal identity to those who are His very own. You are so delightful to Him that He couldn't just give you one name, but He has generously given you a large and compelling identity. Not only has He named you "light" and "salt," but He has given you other names as well!

You Are the Apple of God's Eye

As a young girl, I was always the consummate "Daddy's girl." My father and I looked alike and were interested in the same things. I just couldn't get enough of my dad! When he was in the garden weeding and hoeing, I was his shadow. When he arose early in the morning, before it was light, to read his Bible, I crept down the stairs to be with him. When he watched *Gunsmoke* on TV, I snuggled beside him on the blue velvet couch.

I never felt like he was too busy for me, even though he was a man with a diligent work ethic. No matter what he was engaged in, my dad always had time for conversation with me and for the laughter that we shared. He never tired of my endless questions about the Bible, about cooking, and about gardening. He always made me feel as if I was the most important person in the world.

One day, while I was still in elementary school, my mom said to me, "Carol, you are the apple of your daddy's eye. Don't ever do anything to disappoint him, because it would break his heart." The words my mom spoke to me were not a threat, but they served to remind me over the years how important it was to honor a man who loved me so dearly.

I took delight in being the "apple of my daddy's eye." Because I knew that being the apple of his eye was my precious identity, I never would have dared to disappoint him or to question his loving authority.

You might be tempted to stop reading right now because you grew up with an angry father or with a dad who never took the time to encourage you. Or, your father may have abused you from the time you were a little girl. Let me tell you that your Father story is far from over. You are a "Daddy's girl," whether you realize it or not. You have a heavenly Father who loves to spend time with you and who longs to deposit all that He is into your wonderful life filled with potential.

If you grew up with an unkind or abusive father, or if you didn't have a father present in the home, you especially need to read this chapter. Although your memories might be sad, your future can be filled with hope and joy. You have a Dad who guarantees it because you, my friend, are the apple of His eye!

Keep me as the apple of the eye; hide me in the shadow of Your wings. —Psalm 17:8

This cherished and intimate phrase, *"keep me as the apple of the eye,"* will be difficult to comprehend unless you understand its origins. A more literal translation of the phrase is, "Keep me as the little man of the eye."

Have you ever been in eye-to-eye contact with someone, perhaps having a deep or intimate conversation, and as you gaze into the other person's eyes, you realize that you are able to see your own image reflected in their pupils? Well, you are the "little woman" in the eye of God; He is up close and personal with you. You are reflected in His loving and generous gaze.

You were created for intimacy with Christ. The King of all kings longs to have close and cherished contact with you. Women of all generations have been known to hold Christ at arm's length for many different reasons—perhaps you are one of those women. Maybe your earthly father never loved you or at least never verbalized it, and so you don't believe that you are worthy of love. Or, conceivably, you are dealing with shame over past choices or failures, and so you are afraid to hear what the Lord has to say about you.

Too many women in our culture make the heartbreaking mistake of never living the life of companionship and friendship with God that He has planned for us! Does this situation describe you? You know that you are going to heaven because you have accepted Christ as your Lord and Savior, but you are not experiencing the joy of a relationship with God this side of heaven. You were created to be the apple of your Father's eye, and He longs for you to make time for Him. He is interested in you and in the things that interest you. He is never too busy for you, nor is he distracted by other matters or by "more important" people.

As a young woman, because I knew the value that I had in my earthly father's eyes, I was careful to only make decisions that would honor him or bring pleasure to him. I couldn't stand the thought of bringing even one drop of disappointment to my loving father's heart. So it is with our heavenly Father. When you understand how dearly He loves you and how great is His desire to spend time with you, you will begin to make different choices.

As a woman, if you can comprehend that there is absolutely no one else whom the Father would rather spend time with than you, you will start to choose priorities and activities based upon *His* pleasure rather than upon your own. When you understand how precious your very life is to the

Creator of the universe, your desires will align with His desires. This will never happen, however, until you get close enough to Him to see yourself in His loving gaze.

If you struggle with intimacy with the Father and wonder how to make it happen, let me assure you that it is not "rocket science." Open your Bible to the Psalms and allow the wonder of His presence to wash over your weary soul. Spend some time in worship every day, and even sing out loud as you become better acquainted with your Dad. Expose yourself to powerful and positive Bible teachings through podcasts and books. You might want to buy a prayer journal and begin to write down the sweet thoughts and sayings that your Father is whispering your way. When you welcome the Father into an intimate and loving relationship with you as His favorite daughter, it is then that you are responding to Him as the apple of His eye. Don't neglect this precious part of human existence—don't ignore Him or deny yourself the delight of simply enjoying His companionship. The greatest joy this side of heaven just may be hanging out with your Dad!

You, dear one, are the apple of His eye!

You Are a Champion!

So much of a woman's self-esteem is often dependent upon either the astounding victories in life that she has excitedly won or the tough battles that she has dismally lost. However, we must remind ourselves that self-esteem is not birthed in circumstances, whether they are positive or negative. True self-esteem should always be extracted from the truth of the Word of God.

Yet in all these things we are more than conquerors through Him who loved us. —Romans 8:37 (NKJV)

What exactly are *"all these things"* that Paul, the author of the book of Romans, is referring to? You can discover the answer to that question by reading this earlier verse:

Who will separate us from the love of Christ? Will tribulation, or distress, or persecution, or famine, or nakedness, or peril, or sword? —Romans 8:35

Paul lists some potentially horrible circumstances in life, including *"tribulation," "distress," "persecution," "famine," "nakedness," "peril,"* and *"sword."* In this verse, Paul and the Holy Spirit are reminding us that no matter what happens to us, and regardless of what devastating events we may face in life, our identity remains the same. *"We are more than conquerors"* because of the Savior's great and unconditional love for us.

You were created to overcome circumstances, not to be overcome by them. You were created to conquer difficulties, not to be conquered by them.

Greater is He who is in you than he who is in the world. —1 John 4:4

When you feel that life has beaten you up and you have absolutely nothing to offer in a situation, remind yourself of the One who lives inside of you! When your self-esteem is at an all-time low and you wonder if you can make it through another day, remind yourself of the One who has taken up residence in your ordinary life. You are bigger than all of your problems because of the Christ who lives inside of you! He is the One who gives you strength and your identity as an overcomer. It is not up to you—it is up to Him!

When you are certain that you are going to lose in life and that once again you are destined for defeat, perhaps you should make these declarations out loud:

"I am bigger than all of my problems because Jesus Christ lives inside of me!"

"I have been created by the brilliance of God the Father to overcome in every situation in life!"

"I am destined for victory!"

"Victory—not defeat—is in my certain future!"

On the worst day of your life, when you are shaking with fear and unsure of your calling, remind yourself that you serve a God who has never lost a battle yet, and that He lives inside of you! When you start to believe that you are a champion, when you think those victorious thoughts and declare the power of God over your life, all of heaven lines up behind you and in front of you!

Knowing that the Bible says you are more than a conqueror changes everything for you. It revolutionizes the way you approach problems, difficulties, and disappointments. God will not allow any obstacle in your life that He has not already given you the power to overcome.

I have always deeply enjoyed watching the Olympics. I remember, as a teenage girl, watching people like Dorothy Hamill, Mark Spitz, and Peggy Fleming win Olympic gold medals, and just sobbing as the national anthem of America was played for the entire world to hear.

However, my favorite Olympic event was always the marathon. I loved watching the runners from around the world compete in the grueling 26.2-mile race, which took them through villages, uphill and downhill, and finally through the opening to the Olympic stadium. The entire crowd would jump to its feet and begin to cheer as the frontrunner of the international pack of contestants came into the massive stadium. The champion would inevitably cross the finish line to the glory of a standing ovation and to the earsplitting thunder of the massive crowd.

The aspect of this race, however, that has always been the most fascinating to me was the fact that the champion was never content to merely cross the finish line. The winner would wrap themselves in the flag of their home country and begin to run a final lap around the track. As this extra lap was being run, the crowd would be in an absolute uproar, chanting the name of the victor's country. The thousands of people in the stands would scream for joy and applaud wildly as this one solitary victor ran what is known as "the victory lap."

Every race has a victory lap that is set aside specifically for the victor to run in glory and in recognition of their winning status. The cross of Calvary was the finish line for Jesus Christ, and your life is His victory lap! You get to wrap yourself in the power that belongs only to a Christian and run the victory lap in Him for the entire world to see. Make no mistake about it—the heavenly crowds are going wild, cheering over the life that you are living to honor Him!

You are more than a conqueror in Jesus Christ!

You Are Beloved

For a woman who believes in Jesus Christ, a healthy self-esteem rests on the very simple yet powerful fact that God loves you. That is why you are the apple of His eye! That is why He has made you more than a conqueror! You serve a God who is absolutely head over heels in love with you. You are His first-time-in-forever, and the delight that you bring to His heart is absolutely inexpressible.

I used to tell my children that nothing they could ever do could cause me to love them any less. I was also quick to remind them that nothing they could ever achieve could cause me to love them any more than I already did. What I wanted all five of my children to know was that my love for them was not based upon performance but upon relationship. I was their mom and I loved them.

The Father desires for you to know the same thing: He is your Dad and He loves you.

In the New Testament, in the *New American Standard Bible*, the word "*beloved*" occurs sixty-nine times in sixty-seven verses. The word is used nine times to describe Jesus Christ, God's only Son, while it is used sixty times to describe God's precious and unconditionally loved children. The same word, "*beloved*," that God spoke from heaven to describe how He felt about Jesus, He used nearly seven times more often to describe how He feels about you.

*And a voice came out of the heavens: "You are My beloved Son, in
You I am well-pleased."*   —Mark 1:11

When God the Father spoke these endearing words to His Son, Jesus
didn't argue with His Father or question His motives.

Jesus didn't say, "Oh, Dad, if You had really loved Me, You wouldn't
have put Me here with these people who don't care about Me and who
mistreat Me."

Neither did Jesus respond to His loving Father by protesting, "I am
not worthy of Your love! Surely, You love someone else more than You love
Me!"

Instead, He received the words that His Father had spoken over Him
and walked in His God-ordained destiny from that moment forward. He
loved difficult people and believed for miracles. He provided for others and
taught God's Word. He went about doing good and held children on His
lap and blessed them.

When you believe that you are unconditionally and enthusiastically
loved, you, too, will walk in your God-ordained destiny. You won't be
afraid to dream big dreams or to pray incredible prayers.

It is time for you to extract your self-esteem from God's exuberant love
for you, rather than from the negative comments others may have spoken
over you or the hurtful actions they may have committed against you. If
your family has rejected you, remind yourself that God declares you are
worthy of His love. If men have abused you, remind yourself that God loves
you beyond measure. If your friends have laughed at you, gossiped about
you, and even mocked you at times, remember that the Father treats you
according to His perpetual love for you.

Often, when we don't understand something, we reject it as a fact. You
are loved by the Creator of all things, and even if you don't understand or
believe that reality, it does not change the fact that it is, indeed, a fact! I
have never understood calculus, but that doesn't mean it isn't a valid field of

mathematics. I have never been able to wrap my mind around the Russian language, even though I diligently studied it in college, but that doesn't mean the language is nonexistent!

The fact remains: God loves you, whether or not you understand it or believe it. He loves you infinitely, and you can build an identity on His love! You are the desire of His unending affection. The fact that others have mistreated you or rejected you doesn't change His gargantuan love for you. If your parents didn't want you, or your siblings didn't like you, it still does not negate God's opinion of you.

You, dear one, are His beloved!

Identification Papers

I travel often, and when I am going through airport security in order to board either a national or international flight, I must have my identification papers ready to display. Generally, I travel with a passport and open it to the page that shows my picture and states my name and date of birth. The security agent will study my picture and then look me in the eye to make sure that my face matches the identity I have presented to him.

You have been sent on a holy mission that is not for the faint of heart! God has you on earth at this moment in history for His divine purposes and plans. Do you have your identity papers with you as you travel? Are you ready to show the world your true identity in Jesus Christ?

You must determine not to form your identity upon the systems of this world but upon the kingdom of God. The truth is, we really don't belong here, do we? We were made for another world. However, we have been sent here by our good Father to bring the culture of the Tree of Life to planet earth. We are here as the women of God in the twenty-first century to deliver the nature and character of the Father. We have been given this incredible assignment to shine His light and sprinkle His salt while our feet are on terra firma!

Our knowledge of who we are is extracted from the culture of God. Our job description is found in His Word, and we will carry out His plans until we join Him in eternity. While we are here, we walk by faith and not by sight because our eyes are firmly fixed on a different world altogether. This present world does not issue our identity papers. They have been issued by a kingdom that is unshakable!

You are exactly who God says you are. Now, believe it!

⌒

"Down through the years I turned to the Bible and found in it
all that I needed."
—*Ruth Bell Graham*

PART FOUR

You Are...Never Alone

20

The Loneliest Number?

Many women's lives are saturated with busyness, interactions, relationships, social media, and the expectations of others. However, all of the busyness in the world doesn't guarantee that a woman will never be lonely. Sometimes, the loneliest people of all are young mothers whose lives are filled with the constant tugging of little ones and who rarely experience rich conversation, a pat on the back, or an encouraging word.

Women who are dealing with the empty nest can experience excruciating loneliness as well. When my last child went off to college, I remember thinking, "Will I ever do anything as significant as being a mom?" My nest was empty, my heart was grieving, and my days were long. Loneliness reared its forlorn head in my life.

Widows are understandably lonely, as are single young women. The weariness that ensues from constantly making decisions alone, eating alone, arranging to have appliances or cars repaired alone, and going through the holidays alone can be paralyzing. The absence of a life's companion can carve out a place of pain where loneliness uncomfortably takes up permanent residence.

According to a recent study in *Forbes* magazine, one of the biggest challenges that women in the workforce face is building a sisterhood. This study cites how important it is for women to support and empower one another, especially in the business world. Such a foundational network starts with the basic principles of who we are—our morals, values, and integrity.[7]

Loneliness Defined

Loneliness is simply feeling as if no one sincerely cares about you or is interested in your life beyond surface interactions. It is assuming that nobody desires to listen to your thoughts or quietly understand what is going on in the recesses of your heart. Loneliness might be identified as believing that even if you did have a friend who knew your whole heart, they probably wouldn't like it or accept it.

There is no lonely like walking and patting a colicky baby in the middle of the night lonely.

There is no lonely like another Valentine's Day all alone lonely.

There is no lonely like watching your last child drive out of the driveway to start a life on their own lonely.

There is no lonely like signing the divorce papers lonely.

There is no lonely like walking away from a freshly dug grave lonely.

There is no lonely like eating meal after meal all alone lonely.

If loneliness is not recognized and lovingly healed, it will certainly be the precursor to depression. And when loneliness and depression join forces in a woman's life, it can be a lethal combination of poisonous warfare.

The Backstory of Loneliness

Loneliness is common to men and women of any generation, so it is not surprising that it is addressed in one of the earliest chronicles of human

---

7. Forbes Coaches Council, "15 Biggest Challenges Women Leaders Face and How to Overcome Them," February 26, 2018, https://www.forbes.com/sites/forbescoachescounc il/2018/02/26/15-biggest-challenges-women-leaders-face-and-how-to-overcome-them/.

history—the Bible. In order to understand the particular biblical account of loneliness that follows, we first need to look at its backstory.

Many of the chapters in the Old Testament that precede the book of Psalms depict warfare, including battles of good versus evil and right versus wrong. In His eternal goodness, God was infiltrating an extremely barbaric culture with His name and with His ways. He was introducing His commandments and His benefits to a sinful, prideful group of early human beings. God's *will* was never for human beings to kill one another, and, as you probably already know, that is what He told His people through the leader Moses:

Thou shalt not kill. —Exodus 20:13 (KJV)

Often, when I read the books of the Old Testament, I wonder why the Holy Spirit chose to place these graphic battles of human slaughter in the Bible. I believe that one of the reasons why relentless battles are recorded is that they are symbolic of what we can expect of life this side of heaven. As I read these books of Bible history, I am reminded that I, too, have an enemy who desires to brutally destroy my life and even to kill me. My enemy does not fight fair and is deliberate, barbaric, and ruthless. Also known as Satan, or the Father of Lies, he has one goal, and that is to ruin any hope that I have of living an abundant life. He is not able to take eternity away from me, so he claws and grabs at my emotional life in a desperate attempt to paralyze my heart. Loneliness is one of the many defeating schemes that the enemy uses to devastate a woman's abundant life.

Eavesdropping

Let's listen in now on a private conversation between two Old Testament figures, Ahitophel and Absalom, who were plotting to kill King David. Ahitophel was formerly one of David's closest advisors, but he chose to turn his back on the king and betray him. Absalom was David's own son! Because he knew King David so well, Ahitophel gave advice to Absalom concerning how to defeat and then kill the king.

I will come upon him while he is weary and exhausted and terrify him, so that all the people who are with him will flee. Then I will strike down the king alone. —2 Samuel 17:2

Isn't that both a horrifying and an amazing piece of biblical history? King David's enemy knew that if he could get the king alone, he could strike him down.

Your spiritual enemy has a strategy for how to defeat you, and it is not much different from that of Ahitophel's insight. Satan's goal for your life is to keep you weary and exhausted every single day of your existence. Although he doesn't possess any wisdom, the enemy does have "street smarts." He is wily and beguiling and knows exactly how to magnify the pangs of loneliness in a believer's life. He can grip a woman's heart with loneliness when she is also dealing with weariness, exhaustion, and fear.

Your adversary's focused goal is for you to become distracted by weariness and exhaustion, so he can add fear to your emotional equation, quickly followed by loneliness. Loneliness is real and pervasive. And because it comes at a woman from many different fronts, it must be attacked with different weapons. The first and foremost weapon with which to come against loneliness must be the Word of God. As you battle this wicked emotion, you must attach yourself to the promise that your heavenly Father is with you!

There is power in God's Word to fight every negative emotion and to dismantle the schemes and plans of your archenemy. The devil's subtle whispers shout most loudly when we are alone. Although you may *feel* alone, you must remind yourself that you are never really alone because God promises it:

I will never desert you, nor will I ever forsake you.
—Hebrews 13:5

THE LONELIEST NUMBER? 179

If you are dealing with loneliness today, let these powerful and timeless words from Hebrews bring comfort to your damaged heart. You serve a God who will never leave you alone. You are not forsaken in any situation or at any moment in life. He is with you: what glorious relief! The enemy wants you to believe that you are alone, but according to the Bible, the greatest book of truth in all of history, you always have Someone by your side.

A time of loneliness is one of those strategic moments in life when you must remember that your feelings often do not tell you the truth:

The heart is more deceitful than all else and is desperately sick; who can understand it? —Jeremiah 17:9

Whenever your heart tries to convince you that you are all alone and that no one cares about you or your life, you must once again choose to believe the truth of the Scriptures rather than the instability of your feelings. When it comes to loneliness, you must open your Bible and agree with the Word of God and not with the emotions that threaten to alienate you.

The Last Word

Some days of life are just more memorable than others—there are some events that are seared upon your heart in a tangible and permanent way. Each day that I sent one of our five children off to college holds singular and dynamic memories for me. I cried for weeks dreading the event and then planned, times without number, what my very last words to that precious child would be. How do you express eighteen years of love, laughter, and lifelong lessons in one sentence or less? Should I remind them to brush their teeth every morning? Should I tell them one more time about the day that they were born? Should I talk to them about their spending habits or moral choices? What would my last words be to this person who had grown inside my womb and was now leaving my nest?

I had planned to say great, momentous words—but each time, in the final moment, all I could say was, "I love you. Read your Bible." Still, those two simple sentences were spoken with great heaving sobs and were nearly unintelligible. Even now, as I write these words, there are tears streaming down my cheeks.

Immediately before He ascended into heaven, I wonder if Jesus went through emotions similar to the ones I did when I sent my children off to college. Now, I know that He is fully God and that He knew what was ahead for all of us in heaven—I know that. But don't forget that He was fully man, as well, and He was leaving His "children," His disciples, in a war-torn, sin-filled world.

I can imagine that Jesus and the Father had planned specifically what He would say as He left His band of brothers. What would be the one, lasting sentence that their Lord wanted them to remember every moment of every day? I believe Jesus also knew that the final words He spoke on earth would echo through the centuries and find their resting spot in your heart and in mine.

The final words that Jesus spoke to His disciples were specifically and lovingly chosen to remind them of His perpetual presence. He assured them that even though they would no longer be able to see Him with their human eyes, He would undeniably be with them always!

I am with you always, even to the end of the age.

—Matthew 28:20

The words that Jesus spoke to His disciples are as true for us today as they were for His followers then. He is with you. Remind yourself of that truth in your darkest hours.

They're Playing Our Song

The mournful ballad that the enemy croons over your life is, "One Is the Loneliest Number." Yet the love song that Jesus sings to a lonely daughter is, "You'll Never Walk Alone."

You must gather yourself together, put some resolve in your gut, and remind yourself emphatically that the lie Satan vomits up might twist your feelings, but it is not a spiritual reality. The biblical reality is that you are surrounded by God's love and care every day of your life. Nothing can separate you from the love of God (see Romans 8:38–39); you are securely encircled by His loving care. He has promised it.

There is a friend who sticks closer than a brother.
—Proverbs 18:24

Jesus really is your Best Friend, so feel free to talk to Him anytime… or anywhere. Share your heart with Him and then listen for His loving response. Serve Him everywhere you go and don't forget that you will never be able to out-give Him, although it is a whole lot of fun to try!

Make dates with Jesus. Don't just "pencil" Him in but make a specific date and then keep it! Spend an entire evening in His presence, with worship music playing and the Word of God open before you. Write Him long love letters and sing to Him from your heart while you are in His presence. I have actually been known to enjoy a good laugh with Jesus, and I must tell you…I love spending time in His arms, dancing the night away! When you begin to respond to Jesus as you would to a friend, your loneliness will slowly begin to ebb away.

Sing It Away

Feelings are famous for throwing those infamous pity parties rather than for dealing with the undeniable truth of the Scriptures. What those devastating feelings do is to invite you to come to the party—as the only guest. While your feelings may tell you that you are all alone, let me remind you that the Bible clearly instructs believers how to access the presence of God. The enemy wants you to focus on your feelings, but God says to focus on His eternal truth, making it the foundation of your life.

In my seasons of loneliness, I have reminded myself numerous times that there are at least two ways that will help me walk through the door to God's undeniable presence: fellowship and worship.

For where two or three have gathered together in My name, I am there in their midst.   —Matthew 18:20

This Scripture teaches us that when believers are with each other, He is with them also. If you want to spend time with God, try spending an evening with a group of people who love Him. If you feel alone, invite some people over who love to pray, and guess who else will walk in your door? Find a small group Bible study or a church where the presence of God is real and cherished.

The second way that lonely people can place themselves in the direct presence of the Lord is through the choice to worship.

But thou art holy, O thou that inhabitest the praises of Israel.
                                                        —Psalm 22:3 (KJV)

God dwells where praise is full and strong! If you long for your loving Father to make Himself known and manifest in your life, then you should spend time worshipping Him. The Lord shows up when a man or woman of God rises above events and circumstances with a heart that is overflowing with pure worship. If you deal with loneliness, turn up the worship music and then lift your hands in the air because He is there! You are not alone. Sing out loud and sing out strong! He is there! Sing in the car and make a melody in the shower, and He will be with you. Whenever you have made a conscious choice to worship, you have just placed yourself in His presence.

You can sing loneliness away when you take your eyes off your circumstances and place them on Jesus, who has promised to stay closer than a brother or a sister. You can usher loneliness right out the door when you attach yourself to the unmatched joy of worshipping!

I have a feeling that some of you lonely women are rolling your eyes at me right now, and you might believe that these are ridiculous ways to assuage the pangs that are unique to loneliness. However, let me just tell you that baby steps in the battle to fight the heartache of alienation are all that it takes. Take just one small step toward the Lord today and watch the miracle unfold in your heart!

⌒

"Bare heights of loneliness...a wilderness whose burning
winds sweep over glowing sands, what are they to HIM?
Even there He can refresh us, even there He can renew us."
—*Amy Carmichael*

21

Jesus with Skin On

How wonderful it is to know that Jesus will never leave us or forsake us! The assurance that He is always with us just might be the loveliest and most comforting promise in the entire Bible.

But honestly, if you are anything at all like me, there are some moments in life when you just simply ache for "Jesus with skin on." There have been situations where I felt isolated and just needed another person to touch me. There have been circumstances of solitude where I have throbbed with the desire for someone—anyone—to audibly say a few kind words to me. Please don't misunderstand me. I certainly had the sweet reassurance that Jesus was indeed with me. But oh, how I longed for just one empathetic squeeze of the hand from a friend who cared about me!

During such moments, I have had to learn that it was up to me to reach out. If I was alone, there was a reason for it, and generally the reason was me. I needed to relearn the lesson of maturity that my parents had taught me decades earlier: *If you need a friend, then* **be** *a friend.*

Just Do It!

I am not a doctor, and I am quite certain that I don't have the requisite qualifications to even apply to medical school, much less make it through the exacting courses and training. However, although I don't have the education to match my experience—I am not a certified counselor, nor do my credentials of being a pastor's wife for forty years earn me an impressive degree—I do believe that, in some humorous way, I might be considered to be a doctor of the soul. I have boatloads of experience in administering wisdom to the human heart! So, I hope that you will accept the prescription that I have written to assuage your loneliness.

My prescription for your lonely soul is this: make an assertive and definitive attempt to reach out to someone else at least once a day. If you are still uncertain about what this might look like, read on.

Give to someone else in a kind manner as often as you are able. Don't even pray about it—just do it. Your loneliness will be cured when you find that you are more concerned about someone else's needs than about your own solitary and miserable state of existence. This is not as difficult as you might think at first. Begin by just smiling at a fellow shopper in the grocery store aisle or striking up a conversation with someone while you are in line at the post office. Write a note to an old college friend and reconnect with her. Bake some cookies and take them to a young family from church. Call someone from your Bible study that you'd like to know better and make a coffee date with her. Ask your pastor if there is anyone at church who is also dealing with loneliness and make a plan to get together with that person. Encourage a young mom by telling her that she is doing a good job. Invite a widow out to dinner on a Friday night. Knock on your neighbor's door with a new magazine or a treat from the bakery.

Go out of your way to simply be a friend.

Passivity is not a remedy for loneliness. So, don't grovel in your solitary pain while staying at home watching television with a box of tissues by your side. You have the power to proactively change your life, knowing that the choice to give to someone else is always the cure for loneliness.

It has been said that a person is able to change a habit if they can establish a new discipline for twenty-one days in a row. For some people, it will take longer, and for others it will take less. But I dare you to give something to someone else every single day for twenty-one days, without missing a day. I believe that this may be just the change you have been searching for! You may discover that you have become "Jesus with skin on" to a world in pain.

New Habits

When I was a freshman in college, I was morbidly homesick the entire first semester. I was attending a well-respected Christian university, but it was more than one thousand miles away from my safe, loving home. I did not want to go back to the university after Christmas break, but my father made me return, reminding me that in our family, we finished what we started. My father was compassionate but firm with me.

I begged, with tears streaming down my face, to stay in the safety of my childhood home. My sweet mother was ready to let me stay home and never go back again, but my father, who was wiser and more aware, kindly told me that if I was still unhappy at the end of the year, I could attend a college closer to home for my sophomore year. So, I returned to the far-flung university with a semester's supply of tissue in my suitcases!

One winter evening in mid-January, I was crying in my wing chaplain's room, telling her how lonely I was and how much I hated living away from home. Tanya, who was only one year older than I, was quietly writing something on a piece of paper while I was sobbing and gulping. Honestly, when I look back at the situation now, I realize that I was approaching near hysteria. (Can you tell that the younger "me" had a flair for the dramatic?) When I finally calmed down, she quietly handed me the piece of paper, which had a list of assignments on it:

1. *Do not walk with your head down as you cross campus. Look people in the eye and smile.*

2. *Leave the door to your room open—don't close it.*

3. *On Friday evenings, make popcorn in your room and let the smell waft into the hallway.*

4. *Don't stop at the desk and look to see if there is a note for you. Write someone else a note every day.*

5. *When you go to the cafeteria for dinner, you are not allowed to sit alone. Find a group of people, ask if you can join them, sit down, and introduce yourself. Enter into their conversation.*

Tanya knew that I had developed some horrible habits during my fits of homesickness, and her goal was to break me of the unhealthy social choices I had been making. The list was only the beginning of her remedies because, as I walked out of her room that night, she handed me her popcorn popper and an entire box of stationery to ensure that I would follow through on her to-do list.

The first time I walked into the cafeteria after having been given my life-altering commandments, I found a table where a young man and young woman were sitting together and shyly asked if I could join them. I recognized them as important upperclassmen and thought, "If I can build a friendship with them, I might be important someday, too!"

The young woman hesitated but finally said, "Sure," and the young man just looked away. I could immediately tell that I was unwanted, but I didn't know how to gracefully excuse myself. I wolfed down my dinner in five minutes flat, picked up my tray, and mumbled some incoherent phrase about having to meet someone. Yeah, right…if only I knew someone to meet.

After that embarrassing moment, I felt like a failure and more lonely than before.

A couple of days later, that senior girl came looking for me and knocked on my open door. I invited her in and we sat down to visit. She told me that when I had approached their table, the young man (with no manners!) had been breaking up with her. She apologized for her rude behavior and asked if we could have dinner together that night in the cafeteria. We actually became sweet friends, and I have looked to her often over the years for wisdom and support.

The challenge that we all face is that of vulnerability. When you reach out in friendship to someone, you take the risk of being rejected, and that is always a possibility. There are few things that are certainties in this life, but one of them is this: you will make friends when you become a friend. If you are lonely, instigate a friendship with someone who is lonelier than you are. Listen to someone else's pain rather than talking about your own.

The Remedy

You can feel lonely without really being alone. We all know married women who ache with loneliness, as well as young mothers with a houseful of children who feel alienated and abandoned. You may know popular teenagers who struggle with desperate loneliness. Loneliness is not so much about a lack of relationships as it is about a need to build healthy relationships.

You will conquer your loneliness when you learn how to give while everyone else is living a self-centered and selfish existence. You will no longer feel abandoned if you can learn the secret of being assertively friendly when everyone else is merely passive, or by having a cheerful, positive heart when everyone else seems uninterested. Remind yourself on a daily basis that love is something that you *do*, not something that you feel. If you can reach out in love and kindness to someone every day, regardless of how you feel, it will change your life.

The startling truth that I learned during that companionless first year of college was that the remedy for my empty heart did not lie in the hands of others. It had been in my hands all along. Now, I remind myself every morning that I have been granted another day of living, and I have been given the privilege to reach out in kindness and love to the people whom I meet that day. Who knows? My smile or act of generosity might be an answer to their heartfelt prayers. We really do belong to one another, and that may be the greatest gift of all!

⌒

"You can't always see God's purposes in every season but you
can always have His peace, His presence and His promises."
—*Christine Caine*

22

A Season of Ice-Cold Loneliness

The Creator God, whose genius designed diamonds, orchids, and zebras, also created you with beautiful facets, resplendent fragrance, and unique markings. One of the amazing aspects of your life as a woman is that He wired you for fellowship and for companionship. God established you to desire healthy relationships with others who will encourage you, and whom you, in turn, are given the opportunity to encourage. It's a beautiful, mutual give-and-take of human heart, caring, and compassion. When you are down, you need a friend or family member to pick you up. When you have something exciting or difficult to share, you need someone who will listen and respond with caring words. When you have a prayer request, you need someone to meet with who will pray fervently for you.

It is not a sin or a sign of weakness to desire the companionship of other people—it is simply the way that you were made. God Himself acknowledged this human need as early as the Garden of Eden:

Then the LORD *God said, "It is not good for the man to be alone; I will make him a helper suitable for him."* —Genesis 2:18

In this verse, the Lord notes the man's need for a woman in his life, but we can clearly see that loneliness was never the plan of God for any of His glorious creation of mankind, whether male or female. We weren't created to be alone—we were created for companionship. No woman is an island, able to go through life without conversation, shared laughter, and sweet friendship. So, if you are lonely, even though you are never alone because of the promise of God's presence, you can rest assured that you were designed by your Creator to interact with others. Remember, it is not a sin to desire close friends who will cheer you on through life—it is part of what makes you a glorious creation of the Father.

Don't Waste Your Loneliness

A few years ago, my husband and I realized that God was calling us to make several major changes in our lives. Our youngest daughter, Joni, had just graduated from college and was off to the mission field. Our other four children were flung across the continent of North America, and we found ourselves alone much of the time. Craig was pastoring a thriving church and was busy with meetings, counseling appointments, and overseeing a growing staff. I was writing books and articles, teaching a vibrant women's Bible study, and recording podcasts and radio shows, as well as traveling and speaking. We were very fulfilled in our callings and were even too busy on most days. We knew that we were both being used by the Lord, but we were also aware that we were in a season of stark, solitary living.

During those days, we prayed, conversed, and pondered together, and we heard the voice of the Lord give us clear direction. We both recognized that God was calling Craig to turn the church over to a younger pastor, and we were also in agreement that the Lord was calling my husband to go full-time with a particular missions organization. Craig has always had a heart for the church around the world, and he had recently partnered with an organization that plants churches and trains pastors in India and Nepal. We had heard God's voice clearly that Craig should work with them, so we were excited—even giddy—to move ahead in His plans and purposes.

We had known for years that we would eventually give over the church, which we had planted, to an amazing young couple who were a son and daughter in the faith to us. The timeline was set, and we were moving into the next season of our life as a ministry couple who passionately followed the will and purposes of God! What could go wrong with this plan? It was amazing in every way! Surely, this would be easy, right? Surely, because God had spoken, everything would just flow quickly and there would be no wrinkles, right?

We put our beautiful home on the market so that we would be free to move to the city in which the missions organization's headquarters was located, which also happened to be where three of our five children lived at the time. We fully expected the house to sell quickly because we lived in a region of the country that was a seller's market.

However, our house was still on the market after three months, and it was time for Craig to move to the new location, which was twelve hundred miles away from our western New York home, so that he could lead the missions organization effectively. I had to stay and care for the family home until it sold. Certainly, it would be sold by Christmas!

September and then October passed, with not one offer on our well-cared-for home, which was located in a lovely neighborhood in a sought-after school district. I went to visit Craig once during those two months. One of our sons, who had been living in the city where we were moving, announced that his wife had been offered a ministry job in another state, and they had decided that God was leading them there. So, now we were down to only two of our five children living nearby, but that was okay with us. We just couldn't wait to be with at least part of our family.

In the glory days of autumn, I went for walks by myself and proactively made lunch and dinner appointments with friends who were a great comfort to me. Then came the month of November, with the holidays looming. Craig's salary had changed drastically during this time, and we were quickly going through our savings in order to make the house payment every month. We decided that I would stay in New York for Thanksgiving but join Craig and our other family members for Christmas. I spent Thanksgiving Day in a restaurant with two close friends. There were some tears, but I believed that our house would soon sell and I would be free to move on.

The day after Thanksgiving, although I didn't buy a Christmas tree, I did put up some of my most meaningful and well-loved Christmas decorations so that our home didn't seem quite so barren. I invited a single woman from the church to come over and help me decorate. The days were long and cold, but I continued to look forward to that last week in December when we would all be together.

The entire family gathered in Tulsa, Oklahoma, for our amazing Christmas celebration—there were eighteen of us in all! Oh, what fun we had playing games until late at night, wrapping presents, cooking wonderful holiday treats, decorating gingerbread houses, and praying in the New Year. I loved being with my people...with my tribe...with my DNA...with my progeny.

During the first week of January, I drove halfway across the country by myself to return home. We still did not have even one offer on our house, which was in tip-top shape and in a prestigious neighborhood. We were incredulous!

Do you know what it means to spend the winter alone in a large home outside of Buffalo, New York? Dare I remind you of the frigid temperatures, the wicked weather conditions, and the inability to travel even locally many days? The months were dragging by, and I was experiencing loneliness like never before.

If you find yourself in a season where you feel abysmally alone, what should you do? Is there a heavenly assignment list that will help to assuage the throb that is peculiar to the barrenness of living a life on your own? Or, perhaps your life is filled with people, chores, meetings, and appointments, and yet you still feel alone. What should a woman do in that scenario?

During that period of physical and emotional solitude, I discovered two spiritual principles that bolstered me during the long days of "quarantine" that seemed to be orchestrated by my loving Father. You see, not all loneliness is devastating, and not all solitude results in isolation. There are seasons in all of our lives when we must learn how to embrace the quiet of the moment and then to cultivate the purposes of God in the absence of other people.

Alone, but Not Forgotten

During the seemingly interminable fifteen months that I ended up spending in the family home by myself, I was initially haunted by the noise and cheerful laughter of yesterday. I could still hear my girls giggling in the bathroom with their friends and could still perceive the echoes of my boys cheering for their favorite team in front of the TV in the family room. But all of that was gone and would never happen again, so I had a choice to make.

I was determined not to waste a day of the glorious life that I had been given. When I woke up every morning, I would ask the Father to show me His plan for that day. Some days, He gave me a detailed strategy of who to call and how to invest my hours. On other days, although I asked, He was silent.

Even so, during the taciturn days of my confinement, I determined that God would be my constant Companion and my dearest Friend. Although my house was empty, my heart was filled to overflowing with the fullness of all that He is and all that He offers to an ordinary woman. I gave myself to Him and to His nearness as I never had prior to this season of seclusion.

One of the most significant lessons I learned during this time is that loneliness is often a craving for God. What if God has divinely engineered seasons—not a lifetime, but seasons—of detachment in the lives of believers so that we would begin to look for something beyond ourselves and beyond human companionship? Loneliness can be a powerful magnet that propels a woman to seek Him. I believe, without a doubt, that loneliness can be the gateway to greater intimacy with the Savior.

I always turn to the Word of God when I am facing a life challenge. While I was battling cancer, I turned to the Bible. While I was going through a deep depression, the Word became my fount of joy. While I was struggling with infertility, the Bible gave me hope beyond my circumstances. I am a stalwart believer in the fact that God's will is found in His Word. So many people go through life looking for a "sign" when what they need to do is look for a verse!

And so, during this lonely season of my life, it is not surprising that I instigated a study of the words *alone, lonely,* and *loneliness* in the Word of God and virtually squeezed the truth out of the greatest Book ever written concerning this topic. The cry of my heart at that time was also the cry of David's heart in Psalm 25:

Turn to me and be gracious to me, for I am lonely and afflicted. The troubles of my heart are enlarged; bring me out of my distresses. —Psalm 25:16–17

David was a man who knew the discouragement that often accompanies loneliness. In his moment of solitude, he cried out to the Lord for grace and comfort. But there was something else David knew that you and I might overlook—he recognized the fact that loneliness can actually enlarge your other troubles. When you are lonely, a lack of finances can become more devastating. When you are lonely, health issues can seem more daunting. When you are lonely, a missing sense of destiny can appear cavernous. David asked the Lord to deliver him from that place of enlarged distress.

If you are lonely today, remember that loneliness is often a magnifying glass for other pain and troubles. Rather than allowing your loneliness to be the window through which you view the rest of your life, pray the prayer that David did and ask for the grace of God to help you in your current state. When you view your life through God's grace, rather than through loneliness, you will observe His goodness and faithfulness in all of your circumstances. Would you pray this prayer with David and with me now?

Lord, You know how lonely I am. Would You turn to me today? Would You be that Friend who really is closer than a brother? Would You show Your grace toward me? Lord, help me keep my other troubles in their proper perspective. I pray that I can see my life the way that You see my life. I trust You to bring me out of my distresses. Amen.

"Be encouraged to be an encourager. It's a spiritual art that everyone can learn. And mostly you learn by practicing it."
—*Jill Briscoe*

23

Just like Jesus!

"After He had sent the crowds away, He went up on the mountain by Himself to pray; and when it was evening, He was there alone."   —Matthew 14:23

A t times, Jesus sent the crowds away for His own benefit, and it seems reasonable to me that He might do exactly the same thing from time to time in the lives of His children. If you are a mom, you understand this. Children love play dates, they delight in going to the park with friends, and they beg to have the entire neighborhood over for a game of kickball in the yard, but the mother often needs to say, "It's time for your friends to go home. You need some time alone."

If you have ever been the mother of a teenager or a young adult, you especially understand the importance of sending the crowds away! Most teenagers love activity, conversation, and a continuous social life, but that is not the healthiest way to live emotionally. I believe that during the solitary moments in life, we discover who we really are, while prolonged time spent with the crowd often obscures our true identity.

During that long season that I spent alone in the winterscape of the frigid north, I came to believe that perhaps Jesus had been the One who had actually sent the crowds away. I deeply desired to lean into Him, to acknowledge His presence, and to enjoy the solitary time that He had ordained. And I wanted to learn why He had included solitude in His own life and ministry.

As we learn from the example of Jesus concerning the opportunity of loneliness in the life of a believer, we must observe what He did when He, too, was all alone.

And it happened that while He was praying alone....
—Luke 9:18

Immediately Jesus made His disciples get into the boat and go ahead of Him to the other side of Bethsaida, while He Himself was sending the crowd away. After bidding them farewell, He left for the mountain to pray. —Mark 6:45–46

It seems to me that Jesus was in the habit of proactively being alone so that He could spend time in prayer. I believe that we should imitate everything Jesus chose to do during His time on earth, and if it was beneficial for Him to choose to be alone in order to pray, it will be beneficial for us to do the same.

Do you find yourself in an interval of life when you are often alone? Then let me just encourage you to use those uninterrupted hours to pray to the Father. Let me just remind you not to waste this occasion of solitude in which you have the opportunity to get to know your Dad better. This time of seemingly arid living can be turned into a thriving garden of the Lord's presence if you will only choose to pray.

Often, during such periods, instead of praying, we prefer to binge-watch Netflix, read the latest romance novel, talk endlessly on the phone, or complain on social media. Rather than choosing to be with the Father, we choose to spend money, eat vast amounts of chocolate, or bar-hop. What if God has wisely appointed you to a season of solitary living so that you can grow closer to Him? What if God has sent the crowd away from your life so that you are able to experience breakthroughs and miracles in prayer? What if you will never experience the true love of the Father unless you actually spend time with Him?

The first and most remarkable lesson that I learned during my profitable time of aloneness was to fellowship with the One who knows me best and loves me most. I reveled in a vibrant relationship with Him, and nothing has ever been sweeter.

When You said, "Seek My face," my heart said to You, "Your face, O Lord, I shall seek." —Psalm 27:8

Now, when you choose to pray, not only will you bask in the loving arms of the One who created you, but you will also move heaven and earth! What better way to spend your time than to partner with God to make a difference in the world while on your knees? Days and even years of solo moments are never wasted when we choose to pray. Blaise Pascal, the great French philosopher, declared that in prayer, God bestows upon us "the dignity of causality." When you pray, you can actually revolutionize lonely, empty evenings into a life of dignity that bears a cause even greater than yourself. We often mistakenly identify a season of loneliness as a time of insignificance rather than as an opportunity to wield the greatest significance of our entire lives.

The School of Solitude

If you are a believer in Jesus Christ, you have this mandate of God upon your significant life: you are a disciple who is now called to make disciples. And what better time to assertively do so than when you feel utterly alone? Is there a finer hour to obey the Father than when much of the structure has been removed from your life?

Go therefore and make disciples of all the nations, baptizing them in the name of the Father and the Son and the Holy Spirit, teaching them to observe all that I commanded you; and lo, I am with you always, even to the end of the age. —Matthew 28:19–20

These verses, spoken by Jesus when He was about to return to heaven after His death and resurrection, have historically been known in the church as "the Great Commission." This charge, which was given nearly two thousand years ago, has yet to be completely fulfilled. The body of Christ is still in the process of making disciples of all nations.

You might wonder what this ancient command has to do with the wretched loneliness that has engulfed your life today, but hold on—I am getting to it!

There is a divine assignment with your name on it that loneliness is not able to erase. While you are feeling alone, you can either alienate yourself or you can fulfill the plan of God for your life. And isn't it interesting to note that when Jesus gave His disciples this Great Commission, knowing He would not be physically present with them on earth any longer, He reminded them that they were not alone? He is reminding you of the same truth today: when you reach out to others in order to advance the kingdom of God, you will never be alone!

Whose door will God send you to today? Have you surrendered your time in order to make yourself available to Him and become involved in the lives of others? Are you willing for your very life to be the message that others are longing to read?

I believe that although the Bible was written thousands of years ago, it has the impact of the eternal Holy Spirit upon every page. The words of Scripture are not archaic, nor are they outdated. They have a well-defined impact for women living in the twenty-first century. So, remember, if you are a believer in Jesus Christ, you have been assigned to a restorative job. You have been called to tell others about the love of Jesus Christ, and beyond that, you have been called to make disciples.

What Comes Next?

During those unending months of solitude that I was forced to endure, there was another, less important, situation that took place behind the scenes that actually wounded my soul deeply. My husband was no longer the pastor of our wonderful church, and so the opportunity for me to continue to teach the large and vibrant women's Bible study there came to an end. I had to step aside for the new pastor to walk ahead with his vision, which was one of small groups rather than large, midweek meetings. While I used to spend my Tuesday nights teaching the Word of God to hundreds of women, I now spent it at home, flipping through television channels. While I used to spend hours every week poring over the Word of God, Bible commentaries, and Bible dictionaries in preparation for the weekly teaching, I now found those hours vacant.

As I pondered what was next on God's list of assignments for me and how I could use this time to honor Him rather than wallow in self-pity, I came upon this very familiar verse in one of my daily quiet times:

Older women likewise are to be reverent in their behavior, not malicious gossips nor enslaved to much wine, teaching what is good, so that they may encourage the young women to love their husbands, to love their children, to be sensible, pure, workers at home.... —Titus 2:3–5

Some women might toss this verse aside as outdated or old-fashioned, but it showed me what a pool of energy women are for the family of God! God has a plan for women—and it is that we would pour our lives into the lives of other women! Although my nest was empty, I knew that it was time for me to cultivate relationships with spiritual daughters who might enjoy spending time with me. Just as I had come to recognize during my first year in college, I had the sudden awakening that my ability to live a significant life, even during a season of loneliness, lay in my own hands.

I began to reach out to others. I spent long hours with a young woman who had just been through a broken engagement. I invited a single teacher over to my home for many evenings of conversation and food. I spent time with a woman whose heart was devastated because she had just learned that she would never have children, and we prayed and asked God for a miracle. I encouraged a career woman whose life had been upended by unfair treatment in the workplace. I met a woman for coffee who lived in constant pain due to debilitating back issues. I met weekly with a young widow who lived an hour away so we could share the Word together and receive mutual encouragement.

As I began to pour out my life for others, the word *lonely* ceased to exist for me. Oh, I still longed to be with my husband and couldn't wait for our home to finally sell (which it did after eighteen months on the market), but I discovered the vibrant garden of God in the wilderness of life.

And the LORD *will continually guide you, and satisfy your desire in scorched places, and give strength to your bones; and you will be like a watered garden, and like a spring of water whose waters do not fail.*
—Isaiah 58:11

Homework from the School of Solitude

If you know that you have not been handling loneliness well and are open to becoming available for God's higher purposes, may I suggest that you consider participating in these ways?

+ Pray about who God would have you reach out to in friendship and in discipleship.

+ Think about the women who are in your life to whom you could write a note or an e-mail of encouragement.

+ Ask a widow or a single woman if they would like to go out to lunch or coffee with you.

+ Volunteer to babysit for a young couple so they can have an evening alone together.

- Invite someone into your home who has just walked through a difficult event. Spend some time in prayer together.

- Start a monthly prayer group of like-minded women.

- Be a mentor to a younger woman.

- Find an older woman who will mentor you.

- If you are single, remind yourself that you don't need a significant other to lead a significant life.

Who knows? It might be that from this time of loneliness, the most significant work of your life will be birthed. Perhaps the purpose for which the Father has called you to partner with Him will be revealed in those humble days and quiet nights.

It is not for you to know the times or epochs which the Father has fixed by His own authority; but you will receive power when the Holy Spirit has come upon you; and you shall be My witnesses both in Jerusalem, and in all Judea and Samaria, and even to the remotest part of the earth. —Acts 1:7–8

Start in your Jerusalem—which is your own backyard. Begin by loving people sincerely in your apartment building, on your street, and at your office. The deepest needs that you can meet in someone else's life might be met simply with ears to hear, a shoulder to cry upon, and a heart that will pray. This is how significant women respond to a season of loneliness: they obey the wisdom of the Father.

⁓

"There is something wonderfully sacred that happens when a girl chooses to look past being set aside to see God's call for her to be set apart."
—Lysa TerKeurst

PART FIVE

You Are...a Woman of Grace and Peace

24

Can a Woman "Have It All"?

Once you realize that you have been created by God for purpose, and for a destiny greater than you could ever have imagined; when, at last, you wrap your mind around the marvelous fact that you have been made in His very image; and when you recognize that your heavenly Father is always with you so that you are never alone, there is still one remaining issue that is particularly tricky for women to deal with: women of the twenty-first century are expected to spin a multitude of plates. As a result, they are stressed out, worn down, overcommitted, and understaffed! According to a Barna study, 72 percent of all women feel overwhelmed by stress, and for women who still have children at home, this rate increases to 80 percent.[8] What's a woman to do?

Women must begin to realize that spinning plates is a dangerous occupation, and that in the spinning, something might break or someone might

8. "Tired & Stressed, but Satisfied: Moms Juggle Kids, Career & Identity," Barna: Frames, May 5, 2014, https://www.barna.com/research/tired-stressed-but-satisfied-moms-juggle-kids-career-identity/.

get hurt. However, when the plates that you are frantically spinning can be identified as your children, parents, work outside the home, work inside the home, personal development, church, and friendships, you don't dare drop one of those valuable and fragile plates!

In addition to the perpetual spinning of precious plates, there is the enormous challenge of determining how much time and energy you should give to each area of life. For a perfectionist like me, it is hard not to give 110 percent to everything that I do. If my effort level reaches the red zone of only 99 percent, I am tempted to feel like an abysmal failure.

Erin Joyce, a therapist for women and couples, says, "It's been well-documented in our *Diagnostic and Statistical Manual of Mental Disorders*…that prevalence rates for the majority of the anxiety disorders are higher in women than men."[9] With the renewed vigor of the women's movement in the mid-twentieth century, women were convinced that they could "have it all." They were encouraged to climb the corporate ladder, run for public office, earn advanced educational degrees, and, at the same time, raise a healthy family and build a strong, impenetrable marriage. While any one of those endeavors is noble and even admirable, the truth remains that no one, female or male, can do it all at one time.

I often lean into the wisdom of women who have tried to "have it all" and glean from their life experiences. One such woman is Jill Briscoe, a Cambridge graduate, speaker, teacher, author, and mother. This is her wisdom on the matter: "The secret to 'doing it all' is not necessarily doing it all, but rather discovering which part of the 'all' He has given us to do and doing all of THAT."

Diane Sawyer and Me

When I was a young woman trying to figure out which plates I would juggle at any given moment of my abundant life, Diane Sawyer was one of my role models. I don't know what it was about Diane—whether it was her wonderful mind, her captivating communication skills, or her classic

---

9. Kristin Wong, "There's a Stress Gap Between Men and Women. Here's Why It's Important," *New York Times*, November 14, 2018, https://www.nytimes.com/2018/11/14/smarter-living/stress-gap-women-men.html.

grace—that had always intrigued me. I'd always wished that I could spend just one afternoon with her, but felt that was a preposterous idea, indeed!

Then, I heard that Diane was coming to speak at a university in my area. I couldn't resist this once-in-a-lifetime opportunity to see her in person, so I cleared my very busy calendar and was one of the first to arrive. At that time, I had two preschool boys whose very existence demanded oodles of attention, was daily involved at the church that my husband pastored, and taught a weekly Bible study that required hours of preparation. I was also a freelance editor for a publishing company and volunteered about twenty hours a week for an organization that promoted excellence in the lives of young women. My heart was full and my head was spinning. My home was normally a mess, and we ate out way too often, which impacted our budget. I stayed ridiculously behind in laundry, and there were at least twenty unanswered messages on our answering machine at any given time. There were no blank spaces on my calendar for months, and I hadn't had a decent conversation with my husband in many weeks. However, I did somehow find the time to hear this notable woman, who was about a decade older than I, express her prolific wisdom concerning life and vocation.

Diane talked about the books she had read and the people who had influenced her illustrious and successful career. She discussed the values that her parents had instilled in her as a child and the exciting career doors that had opened for her. I was mesmerized—totally besotted. Then, at the close of her heartfelt and vulnerable speech, this astounding and significant woman opened the floor for questions. A local TV anchor was there to field the questions, and she recognized first a college student who was there in jeans and a T-shirt. (I, of course, wanting to impress Diane, was wearing a black suit, white blouse, black pumps, and the expected string of pearls.) This presumptuous, energetic university coed confidently asked, "Diane, you 'have it all.' Tell us—how do you make it work? I want to 'have it all,' too."

Diane paused for a minute with her elbow resting on the podium, and then a soft smile appeared on her winsome face. This was her unforgettable response: "You can have it all, but you can't have it all at one time. For a woman, there are three priorities in life—motherhood, marriage, and career. If you want to live an excellent life, you can only do two of those things well at any given time. If you try to do all three at once, you will fail someone. That is why I have chosen not to have children. I want to build a great marriage and have a lasting career, so I will enjoy my sister's children."

Although I had arrived that night armed with about ten questions that I deeply desired to ask the woman who had achieved heroic status in my estimation, I quietly folded the paper on which my questions were written and tucked it into my stylish black purse. Her words had resonated deeply within my soul, and I recognized that my plates were falling and crashing. It was time for me to reevaluate my commitments and lower my stress level. My choices might be different than Diane Sawyer's were, but I wanted to live with the intention and grace that she did.

You may not agree with Diane's perspective on a woman's ability to "have it all," but rather than become defensive about your capability and calling to accomplish great things, simply use her words to help you reevaluate what season of life you are in and what you, as a woman, have been specifically called to do.

It's Him Again

Do you recall the Scripture that we studied during our assault against loneliness in part 4 of this book? We will look at it again shortly. But let me give you more of the backstory of this important Old Testament verse. Absalom, David's son, intentionally undermined his father's rule as king. Essentially, he set himself up as judge in Jerusalem and began to make promises of what he would accomplish if he were the new monarch. After driving David out of Jerusalem, this desperate son began to lay plans to pursue and attack David's forces. Ahitophel, one of Absalom's chief advisors, gave him this strategy:

I will come upon him while he is weary and exhausted and terrify him, so that all the people who are with him will flee. Then I will strike down the king alone. —2 Samuel 17:2

Like David, we have an enemy who wants to take advantage of our vulnerabilities. The goal of our spiritual foe is to cause us to be in a state of exhaustion and weariness every day of our lives. The enemy knows that if he can keep us distracted by stress, he can steal the "abundant" right out of our life. Stress will rob us of our joy, dismantle our peace, and deny us hope. Stress doesn't have the power to change tomorrow, but it surely does mess up today!

Are you filled with weariness? The word *weary* can be defined as "to be faint; to be worn out; tired, sick, fatigued, exhausted, and out of patience." Perhaps this definition describes the life you are living today. In any case, that is the "you" that the enemy wants you to be. Satan is conniving, deceptive, and secretive, and he will wear you out in any way that he can. The enemy always fights the hardest when he knows that God has something great in store for you. Don't settle for the devil's overwhelming, stress-filled version of life when God has something undeniably wonderful just for you!

The Route to Weariness Is Short

The route to weariness is a short one, and you can arrive at exhaustion sooner than you dare to believe. Stress has a way of piling up in a woman's life until she is unable to make quality decisions, enter into meaningful conversation, or enjoy the life that she has been given.

Many of the women I know are worn out by overspending and overeating; they are exhausted by overcommitting to the wrong things and under-committing to all the right things. Stress is not merely a result of attempting to do too much, but also of spending your time doing things that leave you unfulfilled and empty. As you fill your life with more stuff and busyness, your archenemy, the devil, who wants you to be constantly run ragged and worn out, is laughing hysterically at you, knowing that he has just won this particular battle.

He will speak out against the Most High and wear down the saints of the Highest One. —Daniel 7:25

Satan is wearing down the saints of the Most High God with busyness and "the tyranny of the urgent." Why are you listening to his strategies? Satan knows that you will lose if he can wear you down. What will you lose? I can assure you that you won't lose your eternal salvation, but you will lose your patience and your temper. You will also lose your perspective and your peace of mind. You might just lose your creativity and your daily disciplines. You might even lose the "you" that the Father meant for you to be.

We mistakenly think that it is more important to sign our children up for soccer than it is to place the Word of God in their hearts. We falsely believe that a trip to Disney World is necessary for our children to experience a magical childhood, so we go deeply into debt to make the annual trek. We think that certainly we deserve the newest, the trendiest, and the finest, so we compromise our way up the corporate ladder in order to afford it. We look at our busyness as an invisible badge of honor, and somehow we think that "more" makes us in some way "better." The mistake that stressed-out women make is that they are deriving their value from what they do, rather than from who they are. Remember the truth that Eve quickly forgot: you are made in the image of God! What more could you want?

The devil is an expert in trickery and distraction. He does not normally tempt you with obvious compromise, but his beguiling strategy is to offer things that *seem* good. A temptation is a thought that will move you in a specific direction. Satan will use something that momentarily appears good to call you away from God's eternal best for your life.

What "good" thing is distracting you from God's best today? Good things may wear you down, but God's best will always strengthen you and bring peace to your life.

Making Changes

You were not created to be an anxious woman whose life is being frittered away at the altar of busyness. You were created for joy, peace, and eternal impact, not temporary distractions. Perhaps it is time for you to make some much-needed changes in your life. This may require reordering your daily schedule or reprioritizing your time commitments. Ask a friend to help you reorganize your life so you are able to live abundantly and not as a worn-out, run-down shrew!

Often, when I am feeling overwhelmed, I make this declaration to the enemy of my soul: "You are not going to wear me down. I am going to wear you down with worship and the Word of God!" Will you make that declaration too?

Begin to reevaluate your priorities so that you can break the cycle of weariness in your life. Choose to spend time with the Lord rather than talking on the phone or playing computer games. Speak psalms and hymns and spiritual songs over your life rather than spouting opinions and gossip and frustration. Purpose today that you will no longer invest yourself in urgent demands, but will devote yourself to important, eternal disciplines. Trust me, you will only need to make a few strategic choices to replace your weariness with God's perfect peace.

The Sweet Place of Abiding

Abide in Me, and I in you. As the branch cannot bear fruit of itself unless it abides in the vine, so neither can you unless you abide in Me. —John 15:4

God has an antidote for weariness. He has prescribed the secret of "abiding" in Him to heal your tired and exhausted soul. The spiritual opposite of weariness and stress may be described as the restorative simplicity of abiding in Christ. Strength always comes from rest—never from needless, perpetual activity.

I have even discovered that rest is a weapon of warfare against the schemes of the enemy! When I am well-rested in Christ, I find that I am a stronger and more valiant warrior. The enemy's desire is to wear me down, but the Father's desire is to strengthen me with the gift of resting in Him.

We are called to remain in unbroken fellowship with Jesus Christ. This place of abiding in Him is not merely a once-a-week visit. We have been invited to build our very lives around His presence. The welcome mat is always out for you to make God's throne room your true home. His presence is not meant to be just a respite from the storm or a lovely vacation home, but it is designed to be a place in which you can establish your life and then never, ever have to leave! When your permanent residence is the presence of Christ, and when you allow Him to whisper in your ear His wonderful plan for each day and each hour, and even the specific moments of your day, then His glorious fruit will be beautifully and deliciously apparent in your well-watered life. We must find quiet moments in our loud lives to begin to hear the still, small voice of the Father.

The Greek word translated *"abide"* in the above verse means "to last or endure." When you abide in Christ daily by continually filling yourself with the manna of His Word, and when you refresh yourself in the cool stream of worship, you will most certainly outlast the devil and his strategies for your life. As you simply abide in Christ, you will no longer be a woman who is stressed out and weary, but you will be a picture of robust health and cultivated loveliness.

⌐∽⌐

"If we really have too much to do, there are some items on the agenda which God did not put there. Let us submit the list to Him and ask Him to indicate which items we must delete. There is always time to do the will of God. If we are too busy to do that, we are too busy."
—Elisabeth Elliot

25

Overwhelmed

Does your heart ever feel overwhelmed? Perhaps you are disheartened by your inability to meet everyone's expectations and demands. Honestly, there are days in my life when my heart vacillates between being raw with paralyzing frustration and being stimulated by a thousand agitations. Continuously, the floods of demands, disciplines, people, chores, habits, vices, and commitments create a massive quagmire in my life that can only be described by one desperate word: *overwhelming.*

Cry Out to the Lord

David, the worshipper and man after God's own heart (see 1 Samuel 13:14; Acts 13:22), seems to have shared my incompetence at dealing well with all that life dishes out.

Hear my cry, O God; give heed to my prayer. From the end of the earth I call to You when my heart is faint ["overwhelmed" KJV, NLT];

lead me to the rock that is higher than I. For You have been a refuge
for me, a tower of strength against the enemy. Let me dwell in Your
tent forever; let me take refuge in the shelter of Your wings.

—Psalm 61:1–4

Although I do not know what specifically overwhelms you, I can assure
you that while the source of your staggering obstacles may look much different than mine, the answer for both of us is the same:

Hear my cry, O God; give heed to my prayer.

When you are overwhelmed, take it from me and take it from David:
the first thing each of us needs to do is cry out to God. We need prayer
more than we need our circumstances to change. Just going to my infinitely
gracious God, who is lovingly attentive in all of His ways, reminds me that
I am not in charge. There is Someone mightier and more powerful than I
who is well able to bring relief to my mountain of stress.

From the end of the earth I call to You when my heart is faint
[*"overwhelmed"* KJV, NLT].

There is no sin in calling out to God when you are completely and
utterly overwhelmed. In fact, there is a sweet and peaceful sense of fulfillment that comes as you throw yourself into His welcoming arms. The sin
would actually be in turning to other, less-satisfying options. Even when
experience has shown us that such activities do not satisfy, we still mistakenly believe that spending, eating, being entertained, or going to the spa is
what we need to conquer the overwhelming circumstances and events of
our life. These are deceptive distractions, possessing all the healing power
of a miniscule Band-Aid after open-heart surgery.

Let God Lead You and Protect You

Lead me to the rock that is higher than I.

In those moments when life derails and overwhelms us, what we need is for God to lead us. We need Him to take us by our human hands and then guide us with His divine hands to a higher place. He always wisely leads His children to a more secure vantage point than the circumstances of life are able to offer. The benefit of standing on the *"rock that is higher than I"* is that it places me above my circumstances, and therefore I am able to see from heaven's perspective.

One of the most destructive mistakes that any of us makes during moments of overwhelming madness is to be led by our emotions. Anger and impatience will do damage to relationships that may be difficult to repair. I must humbly realize that my emotions often lie to me, but God will lead me in triumph even in overwhelming times...especially in overwhelming times.

For You have been a refuge for me, a tower of strength against the enemy.

When you are feeling overwhelmed, do not focus on what is causing the irritation or annoyance. Turn your eyes away from your circumstances. Instead, set your gaze—and your mind—on the only One who is able to help you! Then, begin to declare who God is. The Lord is your safe place and will strongly protect you against the enemy forces of busyness, difficult relationships, a failing economy, health challenges, false priorities, and anything else. He is more than able!

Let me dwell in Your tent forever; let me take refuge in the shelter of Your wings.

There is no safer, more peaceful place to be than to abide in God and with God. When I linger in His presence and enjoy the safety of His Word, it is then that the overwhelming things of this earth truly "grow strangely dim." When His nearness overshadows all that screeches my name, I am at peace at last. The life that He bestows to a desperate woman such as I is the life that I have dreamed about and longed for.

God's presence miraculously enables me to face another day of the demanding details of daily living. His Word powerfully shields and protects me from the rapid-fire of life's stresses. Prayer helps me to wisely focus on what is eternal and not on what merely stirs up a ruckus.

Perhaps, the next time that you or I find ourselves in overwhelming circumstances, what we should do is run to God and all that He is! I resolve to take a break from this mad, mad, mad, mad world and set my heart where it has always belonged...in Him.

Just a Four-Letter Word

I have heard it said that one of the most powerful prayers a person can pray consists of only one, dynamic, four-letter word: *help*. If you are overwhelmed with everything that is on your to-do list, perhaps you should set aside that list, get on your knees, throw your hands in the air, and cry, "Help!" It's a prayer that God will answer quickly, tenderly, and wisely. When your desperate life collides with the Father's peace, you will experience grace and guidance without measure.

Don't make it harder than it is—simply lay down your agenda and ask for the Father's help. It's what He has wanted all along.

⌒

"I am not sure exactly what heaven will be like, but I know that when we die and it comes time for God to judge us, He will not ask, 'How many good things have you done in your life?' rather He will ask, 'How much love did you put into what you did?'"
—*Mother Teresa*

26

Today, Not Tomorrow

Have you noticed that most women are always in a hurry? We hurry to potty train our children, and then hurry them off to preschool so we can have more leisure time. And yet, when they finally leave home, we long for the days when they used to put their little arms around our necks. Then, we wish we hadn't hurried through those years.

Or, we hurry through the grocery store in the afternoon because we still have to make it to the drugstore, the gym, and the dry cleaner's before 5:00 p.m. Yet, in our haste to check things off our to-do list, we miss the elderly man in the produce department who needs a word of encouragement, and we never even think to help the young mom in the checkout line with three young children and a cartload of groceries.

Hurry has become our addictive pattern in life. We hurry through high school so we can grow up and be an adult—only to become someone who rushes through the decades and ends up in middle age as a tired, weary, uncreative woman who asks, "Tell me again why was I in such a hurry?"

The extravagant and undeniable truth is this: today is the very best day of your life! There is no fuller or grander gift than the undeserved endowment of the present. Today is the moment of miracles. The present holds the certainty of great richness and the assuredness of an existence that is, quite simply, too good to be true! Fall in love with being alive today!

_____

Do not boast about tomorrow, for you do not know what a day may bring forth.   —Proverbs 27:1

_____

As a significant woman, made in the image of God, I am able to choose how much splendor I will squeeze out of today. Will I slog through uncommon minutes and look dull-eyed at all that I have been given? Or, will I embrace the ordinary miracles that reveal their lovely heads in every waking moment?

If our focus is fixed on the remote possibilities of tomorrow, we will never be captivated by the wonder of now! We must keep in mind that stress and its accomplice, weariness, are unseen thieves that will embezzle the joy and peace right out of a wonderful day!

_____

...and tomorrow will be like today, only more so.

—Isaiah 56:12

_____

A Word for Moms

If you are a mom, don't wish your child's life away by saying things like this: "I can't wait till my baby sleeps through the night...is potty-trained... learns to talk...goes to preschool."

Indulge in the amazement of parenting that belongs to you today. When you are up with a colicky baby, pray that this little heart will stay soft toward the Lord and that he or she will walk in their God-directed destiny in life! Don't waste time mourning over lost sleep, but instead celebrate the quiet moments of prayer that are so vital to the person this little life will become.

You can allow stress to dominate these demanding years of your life, or you can intentionally choose to enjoy each day and pray your way through the stress. Treasure every season, every day, and every unscripted opportunity to pour love, time, and training into the child who will become the legacy that you leave behind.

I have heard it said that "motherhood is when the days never end and the years fly by." I know from experience how true that is! Time is a rare commodity, and once it is gone, you can never recapture it or reinvest it. Give yourself a break, mom, and rather than compare your life to other people's lives on social media, choose to splash happily in the life that you have been given. Be generous in praising your little flock and don't allow the unmerited stress in your life to cause you to speak to them in caustic or impatient tones.

When I was in the throes of changing diapers, dealing with the temper tantrums of two-year-olds, and handing out Cheerios, I had a very wise woman tell me that, if you do it right, being a mom to a teenager takes just as much time as being a mom to a toddler. She was correct, of course, and if your brood is now into those infamous teenage years, they need your presence and your peace more than ever. In the years of acne, broken hearts, and driving permits, spend time listening and asking questions. Teenagers can sense stress, and if they think that you, as the mom, are too busy for them, they are likely to shut their hearts to your input.

It is true that whether your child is merely days old or is on the precipice of flying away from the family nest, "love to a child is spelled T-I-M-E." If you don't have enough time to give generously to the lives who are depending on you for stability, affection, and guidance, your priorities must change. They must.

As a mother and as a woman, this quote by Jacqueline Kennedy has always resonated deeply within my heart: "If you bungle raising your children I don't think whatever else you do well matters very much."

"Now"—A Word for Every Woman

It's not only mothers who have the propensity to believe the fantasy that tomorrow holds the treasure that today lacks. Many career women are anxiously awaiting the next big raise, the next incredible bonus, or the next amazing promotion. Many single women, comparing their own lives to the lives of their married friends, spend their time dreaming about finding the right man. They think this will solve all their problems and loneliness. If you are a single woman, let me remind you one more time that you don't need a significant other to lead a significant life.

Women in every season of life must always remember that the choices they make today determine the joy and love they will experience in all of their tomorrows. The investment of whole-hearted engagement in the present will assuredly bring a wealth of resources tomorrow. However, the focus must be on living well *today*.

My mouth is filled with Your praise and with Your glory all day long. —Psalm 71:8

Dr. Steven Garber defines the word *vocation* as "one's entire life lived in response to God's voice." This definition speaks resoundingly to me as a woman, and it applies to any season and every situation of life. Honestly, this definition helps me to cope with—and to dispose of—those wretched spinning plates that have become a serious distraction.

The following is the response of Kate Harris, a mother of three and the leader of an organization dedicated to vocation and calling, to the above definition:

This definition, from my friend and colleague Dr. Steven Garber, is the closest I have come to finding a framework big enough to make sense of my life and work. It gives space for the dimensionality of my identity as a daughter, sister, wife, writer, friend, manager and more. It gives account for the physical work of pregnancy and nursing, while never insisting those wearying months be wholly separate from other efforts such as writing an article during naptime, teaching my other children to read or attending a seminar. This understanding of vocation never makes me choose once and for all between the thrill of crafting a new grant program and the simple joy of visiting with a good friend late into the evening. I can live into my vocation in both places—allowing it to inform the work I do and the kind of friend I am.

Such a definition of vocation will ask me to make practical trade-offs. But vocation never asks me to compartmentalize my life into artificial categories of "work" and "life," or "home" and "market." Vocation offers the possibility that my life and my faith can be richly and imaginatively stewarded as a whole that is far greater than the sum of its parts.

God cares that I steward the life that is in front of me right now. To wrestle and wrangle or muddle my way through it— whatever it takes—but always to insist that it makes sense, that it holds together. To believe the details of our days really do connect to some bigger purpose God has for our lives.[10]

The Beauty of Now

Whenever I am fighting off the monster of stress, and I often do, I have found it invigorating to keep the following declarations close at hand. I choose to lay aside my to-do list and take the time to remind myself—out loud—of the internal and external priorities that are most important for me. Perhaps you would like to spend just a few minutes today to make some declarations that have the power to unlock the beauty and glory of all of the "now" moments of your life:

"Today, I will splendidly and extravagantly spend time listening to others and not merely thinking about me."

---

10. "Tired & Stressed, but Satisfied: Moms Juggle Kids, Career & Identity," Barna: Frames, May 5, 2014, https://www.barna.com/research/tired-stressed-but-satisfied-moms-juggle-kids-career-identity/. Used by permission.

"Today, I will celebrate my current season of life and not foolishly long for different days, experiences, and activities than the ones that have been delivered to my doorstep on this day."

"Today, I will not worry about what I do not have but will gratefully share all that I do have with the people I meet along the way."

"Today, I will use my best dishes and linen napkins for no reason at all!"

"Today, I will sing without regret and say 'Thank you!' loudly and often!"

"Today, I will smile at children…give words of encouragement to strangers…and respond to the love I have been given."

"Today, I will wrap myself in the glory of creation—whether it is in the sparkling and quiet white of a winter afternoon or in the firefly and watermelon moments of summer. I will deeply inhale the luscious days of new birth that only spring delivers and thoroughly appreciate the color and harvest of an autumn afternoon. Whatever season I am in…that season will be my favorite!"

"Today, I will be the very best 'me' I can be. I will cease creating the fantasy 'me' of the future while seeking to fulfill God's true purposes for my life."

"Today, I will make myself at home in the pleasure of this day and find the fingerprint of God in every moment. I will listen for His heartbeat and the song of life that comes only from heaven."

"Today, I will connect myself to the present…and be captivated by the gift of today!"

And my tongue shall declare Your righteousness and Your praise all day long.   —Psalm 35:28

Just Say No

Often, when people ask me to take on yet another responsibility, write another article, participate in another event, or counsel another woman, I say yes simply because I am honored by the request. I am flattered by the attention that is thrown my way by their obvious need of my gifts or abilities. However, I have sadly determined that many of my "yeses" in life have been birthed in pride. And I have learned, over the course of the years, not to say yes to something just because it makes me feel more important. I remind myself that my importance in God's kingdom is not based upon what I do but upon who I am in Christ.

As a woman, and as a fellow traveler along life's busy road, let me encourage you to decide what kind of life you want to live and then to say no to everything that is not that life.

⌒

"Our generation is so busy trying to prove that women can do
everything men can do, women are losing the unique qualities
that set us apart. The God-given femininity and unique way
our Creator designed us. Women weren't created to do
everything a man can do...women were created to
do everything a man can't do."
—*Author unknown*

27

The Stuff of Which Eternity Is Made

As we deal with our stress level by reordering our priorities and cleaning out our closet of commitments, we must be very certain to embrace an eternal mind-set rather than a temporary delusion. Every decision must be made and every priority must be set with eternity in mind rather than with only earth's demands in view. Stress happens when we carry more than God has called us to bear, and when we do more than He has called us to do. Stress is a warning signal that something in our life needs to change.

Stress can also be the result of committing to the wrong things rather than the right things. For instance, if I tell my cousin that we can go on a joint family vacation, when God has called my family to forgo a vacation this year to save money, I will experience stress. It's a wonderful idea to take a family vacation—but not if you have to go into debt to do it! Or, if I commit to volunteer for a civic organization, when God has called me to prepare for a missions trip, I will experience stress. There is nothing intrinsically wrong or sinful about volunteering for an organization—unless God has said, "Not right now."

Just a Few Questions

Twice a year, I purposefully take personal inventory of my time commitments, pausing to reevaluate the activities to which I have dedicated myself. I make time to pray over my calendar and listen for the voice of God concerning the priorities that I have set for my life.

The first time this occurs is during the last week of December and the first week of January. This two-week window is a prime time to identify who you are, who you are becoming, and who you want to be in the New Year. I know one thing for sure and for certain—I don't want to be the stressed-out version of myself! I deeply desire to be a woman whose walk is peaceful and whose purpose is eternal. My family and friends deserve that second woman, not the first one!

The second annual season that I set aside to reconsider the activities that fill my calendar is the last week of August. This is because there is something fresh and new about the first week in September. I am sure that I have mentally attached that time of year to the delight I felt as a young girl in beginning a new year of school.

During both of these times of reevaluation, I prayerfully ask myself a simple list of questions. Perhaps, in order to alleviate stress in your valuable life, you would do well to conduct some self-interrogating also:

1. Does this activity glorify God?

2. Is this commitment a benefit or a deficit to my family and home life?

3. Does this commitment allow me to make an impact for the kingdom of God?

4. Does this activity meet a personal goal that I have set for myself (such as losing weight, learning a new skill, and so forth)?

5. Am I doing this to please people or to please the Lord?

6. Does this activity add stress to my life?

7. Is this an activity that God has for me right now, or is there a different season in life when this activity would be more beneficial for me?

After asking yourself the above seven questions, evaluate your response to each one. Weigh your answers and determine if you should continue with a particular commitment or lay it aside for this season in your life. Again, decide what kind of life you actually want to live and then say a resounding "No!" to whatever isn't that life.

So often, I have made decisions and commitments based on my people-pleasing bent. I long to be known as a "good girl" and have people think that I am absolutely wonderful, and therefore I agree to do something that is simply not God's plan for my life. I have been known to say, "Sure, I'll do that!" when I actually should have said, "Thanks for asking, but it is just not possible for me at this time." As I have matured in who I am as a woman, I have realized that I will never please the world—and what a ridiculous goal that would be if it were even possible!

My Life in My Hands

I wonder how many sermons I have heard in my six decades of living. I have surely listened to thousands of scripturally based, well-thought-out, three-point sermons in my life! I have heard hundreds of pastors, evangelists, and teachers expound on the Word of God, and it has stirred my very soul. I have read books beyond count, written by the greatest theological minds, not only from my generation, but also from generations past. And I wonder how many times I have read the Bible through from cover to cover. How many times have I turned those sacred pages and feasted on the sustenance that only comes from the Scriptures?

After all that, I should know what the Bible says, right? However, I was recently reading my Bible and was absolutely gobsmacked by a particular verse in Psalms that has messed with my theology ever since the day I saw it in a new light.

My life is continually in my hand, yet I do not forget Your law.

—Psalm 119:109

I have always believed that my life was in God's hands—and it is. He is sovereign, and He is most assuredly the God of all authority. Yet He has also given us free will to choose Him or not—to choose well or not. He has given us the power to determine what level of stress we have in our lives. He always offers peace and rest to His children, even in the midst of chaos and busy living. I know that peace and rest are His will for my life. However, I have the option to choose Him or not, and in that respect, my life is in my own hands.

What an extraordinary verse Psalm 119:109 is for those of us who are stressed-out, run-down, and weary all the time! My life is in my hand, and I must listen to God's voice and then choose to obey it when I am determining my time commitments and activities.

Rest—But Don't Quit

As a woman, one of the most important things to remember when you are evaluating all that you do, all that others want you to do, all that your family requires, and all that is urgent, is that it isn't God's will for you to live a life of stress. There will certainly be some seasons that are busier and more demanding than others, but when you partner with God, you can walk through even those days with peace in your heart.

There will be seasons in life when you will have to learn how to rest, but not quit. Only a woman whose heart is centered on eternity will be able to navigate busyness while continuing to keep a calm heart, a peaceful countenance, and a gracious voice. In the most pressured and overloaded times of life, your faith will guide you, keep you, and control you.

"Weary Yet Pursuing"

It's true that in the life of a woman, there will be moments that are demanding and filled with long to-do lists. You will wonder if there are enough hours in a day for you to accomplish everything that is required of you.

Gideon was an extraordinary leader who delivered Israel from the Midianites. He heard the voice of God and obeyed His explicit instructions, leading him to win one of the most compelling battles in all of military history. With God's power, Gideon and his band of three hundred men routed an army of a hundred and twenty thousand, and most of the enemy forces were killed. Immediately after their victory in this unlikely battle, the Lord called Gideon's three-hundred-man army to keep pursuing the fifteen thousand remaining soldiers and their leaders. (See Judges 7–8.)

Have you ever felt that you had just accomplished a long list of expectations, when the Lord called you to one more task? Have you ever wondered where your strength would come from to complete all that God has called you to do?

This is what Gideon and his men did at that challenging moment:

Then Gideon and the 300 men who were with him came to the Jordan and crossed over, weary yet pursuing. —Judges 8:4

There are three words hidden in this verse that have always challenged me in a wonderful and positive way. Have you guessed what they are, my friend? They are the words *"weary yet pursuing."* I believe that there are moments in my life when the Lord calls me to do something that is too difficult for me— or that seems too difficult due to my exhaustion. He often chooses to do this in order to teach me that even in my weariness, He is enough. There are battles that He calls me to engage in for which I must trust Him to give me the needed energy. There are moments when I am drained, but I must continue to pursue God, His victory, His strength, and His plan.

Gideon even presents the recipe that will serve to strengthen us while we are "weary yet pursuing." Let's listen in and hear what Gideon, in his wisdom, asks for in his weariness:

He said to the men of Succoth, "Please give loaves of bread to the people who are following me, for they are weary, and I am pursuing Zebah and Zalmunna, the kings of Midian." —Judges 8:5

When Gideon was pursuing His enemy, he was running out of strength, but he knew exactly what he needed—he needed bread. Bread is what we all need in our relentless pursuit of all that God has for us. I have found that I need the Bread of Life, the Bible, every day in order to stay strong and remain at peace in the overwhelming demands of life. In the midst of your busyness, never forget the sweet nourishment that comes from a daily diet of ingesting the Bread of Life. When you are too busy to read the Bible, you are too busy!

If, like Gideon, you are called to continue to pursue something even though you are weary, you must make the Word of God a delightful priority in your busy life. You must. And God will sustain you. As the apostle Paul wrote,

---

And He has said to me, "My grace is sufficient for you, for power is perfected in weakness." Most gladly, therefore, I will rather boast about my weaknesses, so that the power of Christ may dwell in me.   —2 Corinthians 12:9

Strength in the Midst of Stress

You are stronger than you imagine and are able to do more than you think because you have Jesus alive inside of you. You might feel weak and unable to cope; you might feel like you are letting everyone in your world down. However, those are the very moments when you can ask for God's strength and peace. This is both a mystery and a miracle: when you are at the point of greatest frustration, God is able to fill you to overflowing with His strength and peace.

It is when we get to the end of ourselves that we are more apt to surrender our will, our calendar, and our ways to God because we know that we can't survive without Him. You may be at that point today. If so, you are at the place of a miracle! God loves to infuse weakened and weary women with His supernatural strength and joy. It's what He does best!

If you are at that infamous "end of the rope" today, I encourage you to declare this verse aloud:

I can do all things through Christ who strengthens me.

—Philippians 4:13 (NKJV)

"But God is the God of the waves and the billows, and they are still His when they come over us; and again and again we have proved that the overwhelming thing does not overwhelm. Once more by His interposition deliverance came. We were cast down, but not destroyed."

—*Amy Carmichael*

28

There Is a Place

In seasons of busyness and stress, isn't it reassuring to know that the Father has a better plan for us? God has an all-encompassing solution for busyness, and it's called "peace." He has an antidote for stress, and it's called "rest." While you might feel that your life is spiraling out of control, know that even in the midst of a cyclone of anxiety, there is a place of quiet rest.

I Wonder

When my life has been distorted by busyness and stress, I often think about a series of three verses in the gospel of Matthew. As you read these comforting verses, it's important to remember that Jesus was a carpenter who most likely ran the family business after the death of His earthly father, Joseph.

Come to Me, all who are weary and heavy-laden, and I will give you rest. Take my yoke upon you and learn from Me, for I am

gentle and humble in heart, and you will find rest for your souls.
For My yoke is easy and My burden is light.

—Matthew 11:28–30

The Bible comes alive for me as I try to imagine the context and setting of Jesus's words. A yoke was a heavy wooden harness that fit over the shoulders of oxen and was attached to a piece of equipment that the oxen were expected to pull. It was very important that the carpenter who fashioned the yoke made sure that it fit well and there were no places where the yoke could rub against the shoulders or neck of the oxen and thereby cause painful sores that would be difficult to heal. A carpenter in ancient times also sanded all of the rough places out of the yoke until it was smooth, with no splinters that might injure the beasts of burden.

This phrase *"for My yoke is easy"* can be translated as "my yoke fits well." Would you wonder about this with me for just a minute? Would you try to imagine what the front of the family carpenter shop that Jesus was in charge of prior to His years of ministry looked like? I wonder if Jesus had a yoke over the top of the door on which the words "My yokes fit well" were carved. I wonder if Jesus was known for smooth and well-fitting yokes that farmers could not resist. I wonder....

The truth is, whatever God has called you to do should "fit well" as you walk through life. If you have committed to something that is causing painful sores in your life—mentally, emotionally, spiritually, or even physically—then you can be assured that Jesus has something different for you because His yoke always fits well.

If God Calls You to It

If God calls you to a particular activity or commitment, He will give you the strength and the wisdom to stay faithfully committed to that task. Yet, if you have chosen, apart from the wisdom of Christ, to commit to a particular responsibility, the stress will be enormous.

When you decide to stay engaged in undertakings that you have not consulted the Lord about, it is like a kitten trying to carry what was only meant for a beast of burden. A kitten's bones are fragile and were never meant to carry hundreds of pounds of weight, while an oxen or a workhorse has been especially designed to bear demanding loads. God the Father created you to commit yourself to specific assignments during your tenure on planet earth. Don't kill yourself in the process! Listen for His voice and ask Him to give you the wisdom to decide which commitments are right for you and the strength to follow through. Rather than just "think" about something, take the time to pray about it! Perhaps the following would be a powerful prayer in your life as you determine whether a certain activity or commitment is a good fit for you:

Father, would You show me what to do? I don't want to commit to anything that is not well-pleasing to You and to Your plan for my life. Lord, I pray that You would deliver me from the desire to please people and help me to live a life of productivity, joy, and peace! In Jesus's name, amen.

Commit Before You Commit

There is a glorious freedom that occurs in our life when we commit our ways to God before we commit to another activity or event. When I am in constant communion with Him and when I am daily listening for His voice, I am not chained to the expectations of others but am attached solely to His leading and His desires. Oh, I know that there will certainly be days that are filled from start to finish with endeavors, appointments, and even craziness. However, in the midst of it all, if I am committed to Him, there will be joy and even peace. I will be more aware of His supernatural and soothing presence than I am of the demands of the day.

There is a beautiful sequence of verses found in the book of Psalms that often carries me toward wisdom as I try to determine what the activities of my life should be.

Trust in the LORD *and do good; dwell in the land and cultivate faithfulness. Delight yourself in the* LORD; *and He will give you the desires of your heart. Commit your way to the* LORD, *trust also in Him, and He will do it. He will bring forth your righteousness as the light and your judgment as the noonday. Rest in the* LORD *and wait patiently for Him.* —Psalm 37:3–7

First of all, I must trust in the Lord and in His plan for my life. Secondly, I must determine that everything to which I am setting my hand is something "good" in nature. Jesus went about doing good—and so should I! Every activity in which I involve myself should reflect the goodness of God, whether it is reading to my children, taking my neighbor to a doctor's appointment, or finishing a work assignment.

The third step in this lovely process that leads me toward peace is that I must simply determine that, no matter what the circumstances and regardless of the distractions, I will be faithful. If I said that I will do something, then I must follow through. Faithfulness is an attribute of God Himself, and it is one of the areas in my life where He can show up in power and strength. On my own, I am not a very faithful person because I can make up excuses, feign illness, or pretend that I have forgotten a commitment. Later, however, my dodging of a prior commitment only stirs up mental stress in my life because I feel so guilty for fudging my way out of it. Faithfulness always brings peace, even when it means dying to self.

The next requirement as I travel toward the peace that the Lord has for me is that I must delight in Him—and not in the approval of man. I must remind myself that it is His applause alone for which I live, not for a standing ovation from friends. When I delight myself in God, I discover the deepest desires of my heart. He cultivates ideas and yearnings inside of me that I didn't even know were there before I delighted in Him! How wonderful is that?

And then, before I commit to anything else in life, I must commit myself fully and wholeheartedly to His plans and ways for me. I must understand that what He has for me might be different from what He has for you. But as I commit myself to Him and His ways, a wonderful trust will flood over my soul. I will realize that He is in control, and He will accomplish what concerns me. (See Psalm 138:8.) My capacity to behave in a righteous manner is dependent upon my ability to trust Him, to be a faithful servant, to delight myself in all that He is, and to commit to Him before I commit to anything else.

When I have the first tenets of this passage in order in my life, then my righteousness and my judgments will be strong and wise. The sweet wonder of it all is this: I will be a woman at rest! Who wouldn't want to approach life in this manner?

Those Seasons of Busyness

Let me assure you that even during seasons in which you feel utterly consumed due to the stresses of life, you can still reach this state of peace. Perhaps you are experiencing one of those times now. The college years are perpetually filled with deadlines, classes, assignments, and meetings. The years when a woman is mothering a brood of children who have homework assignments to finish, piano lessons to practice, youth groups to attend, and sports practices to show up for can be intensely overloaded. For a career woman, there will be periods when she feels utterly buried at work due to the demands of the business world. Perhaps you are a caregiver and feel absolutely disheartened and beaten by the unending care of someone you love.

If you can remain peaceful and unruffled when the world is warring around you, you have learned the sweet secret of God's wonderful presence. I have to remind myself time after time, and year after year, that my peace is not dependent upon the number of appointments on my calendar but upon my relationship with Him!

I have a dear friend who is living through the busiest years that a woman can imagine. She has four teenagers—picture that! It seems like she just returns home from a ball game when she must make a costume for a play or plan a party for someone's birthday. It seems that as soon as the school musical is over, it is time to drive a son to a hockey tournament or make sure that a daughter is prepared to take the SAT. In addition to being involved with her children's activities, she is helping to care for both her widowed father and her widowed father-in-law. Besides all this, she works part-time. Honestly, I get dizzy just watching her!

Whenever this friend comes whizzing through my door for a short visit, I always tell her, "Deb, wring the joy out of this day. Believe me when I say that you will miss this season in life. Enjoy every minute of the hurricane and the chaos that is currently your reality. Purpose to have fun in the midst of it all."

It is vital to order your life in such a way that when you make it through a season of breathless busyness, you can enjoy a season of respite. Your body was not designed to live at full throttle for eighty years. You were made with a deep need for rest. Rest will restore and rejuvenate you for the next season of intense activity.

Give Yourself a Break!

What is rest? Is it just a well-deserved and greatly desired nap on a Sunday afternoon? Is it that magnificent week that you spend at the beach every year? Is it the opportunity to put your feet up after a long day of shopping?

Such periods of respite can certainly help. However, rest is actually much more than all of that combined!

Six days you are to do your work, but on the seventh day you shall cease from labor so that your ox and your donkey may rest, and the son of your female slave, as well as your stranger, may refresh themselves. —Exodus 23:12

God created our bodies for a six-day cycle of work, followed by a day of restorative rest. He created animals for rest as well. Did you know that even He took a day of rest, setting aside work after He had created the world in which we live? Because God ceased from His work for a period, and He created us to have built-in times of rest, I have a feeling that your body demands and deserves that rest!

By the seventh day God completed His work which He had done, and He rested on the seventh day from all His work which He had done. Then God blessed the seventh day and sanctified it, because in it He rested from all His work which God had created and made. —Genesis 2:2–3

If God gave Himself a break, so should you. You are not stronger or more adequate than He is. God created your body, your soul, and even your spirit to require periods of refreshing from the onslaught of "Do this! Do that! This must be accomplished! This has to be repaired! This…This… This!"

Come to Me, all who are weary and heavy-laden, and I will give you rest. —Matthew 11:28

Rest is not found in binge-watching a series on Netflix. Nor is it discovered at the spa. Rest is found wherever our heavenly Father is. Rest is found when you come to the Lord with your problems, your trials, and your schedule, and you lay it all at His feet. Rest is the quiet confidence that God radiates to all who will take the time to respond to His call to "*Come.*"

Oh, how I love this definition for the poignant and powerful word *rest* that I once came across!

To cause or permit one to cease from any movement or labor in order to recover and collect his strength.

Are you ready to rest and be strengthened so you can recover from the damage that your busy schedule has done to you? When you choose to go to the Lord, He offers you the sweet opportunity to cease from movement and from labor. Aren't you ready for that? Aren't you ready to lay at His feet everything that causes that dreadful stress? But it is not in the ceasing alone that you find your rest—it is when you collect your strength in His presence. Of course you will find strength in His presence! Strength is there because joy is there! *"In [His] presence is fullness of joy"* (Psalm 16:11), and *"The joy of the* LORD *is your strength"* (Nehemiah 8:10).

Do you see this beautiful progression? My heart is in my throat, and I can barely sit on my chair as I realize what happens when I come to Him! Let me explain it to you in chronological order:

1. I come to Him.

2. He speaks to the busyness in my life and says, "Peace, be still!"

3. I experience the joy of His presence.

4. The joy of His presence strengthens me.

5. I am now rested and recovered from the busyness!

It's only in coming to God that you have any chance at all of living a stress-free life. Even within the onslaught of an exhaustive daily existence, you can have His peace when you determine to come to Him. Doesn't that sound like a perfectly lovely invitation?

Don't worry about anything; instead, pray about everything. Tell God what you need, and thank him for all he has done. Then you will experience God's peace, which exceeds anything we can understand. His peace will guard your hearts and minds as you live in Christ Jesus. —Philippians 4:6–7 (NLT)

One Last Call

If you have an enormously demanding life and are still uncertain if you will ever experience a day that is stress-free, I have one last suggestion for you. I am sure that this recommendation is actually found all over the pages of this book, but in case you haven't heard it clearly before now, let me say it just one more time: if you are living a life of worry, anxiety, busyness, and stress, start to worship your way through every single day. Worship and stress cannot live in the same heart—they are mutually exclusive.

When you sing, anxiety runs away.

When you break out in praise, stress hides its head.

When you worship the Lord, He will give you a clear plan for your life that will always result in peace. I guarantee it!

⌒

"Blessed are the single-hearted, for they shall enjoy much peace. If you refuse to be hurried and pressed, if you stay your soul on God, nothing can keep you from that clearness of spirit which is life and peace. In that stillness you will know what His will is."
—*Amy Carmichael*

Epilogue: You Are…Significant!

My friend, you are not just "good enough"—you are spectacular! You are a unique expression of God's creative genius. Don't ever forget it!

You are not just important—you are a woman of unmatched significance! Your life matters to the purposes and plans of God. If He had not required your presence at this grand celebration known as "life," He would not have taken the time to create you. But here you are—in all of your beauty and value—to make a mark for His kingdom. Please don't lose sight of that astonishing fact!

Just One Woman

I have always felt an intimate kinship with Mary, the mother of Jesus Christ. She was just an ordinary girl, plucked from the safety of her family and the obscurity of her village to live in the magnificent plan of God. Her response to His call on her life has always both amazed and convicted me.

After finding out that she had been chosen to deliver the Christ child to the world, the young mother-to-be didn't worry, complain, or deny His miraculous plan. Mary worshipped her Creator as she entered the house of Elizabeth, her older relative, who was also with child. At this challenging moment in her life, Mary broke out into a rich melody of praise.

Whereas, later, the shepherds were astonished and even frightened by the angelic birth announcement of a Savior, Mary was submissive to God's purposes and acquiesced to all that He had for her. She wasn't tempted to run away in fear, as the shepherds were, but rather gave her entire life for the will and plan of God.

And while the wise men were giddy with explosive joy, Mary quietly treasured all that she was called to embrace in the deep places of her heart.

Perhaps it is time for you and me to learn from Mary's sacred response to the undeniable plan of God for her life. I am in quiet wonder as I hear the Holy Spirit whisper to me, just as the angel Gabriel had declared to Mary, "Do not be afraid, for you have found favor with God." (See Luke 1:30.)

As you finish the final pages of this book, and as you perhaps take a deep breath of resolve, I pray that, with Mary, you will worship, you will submit, and you will treasure these things in your heart.

A Gift

Your identity as a woman is a rare gift, so embrace it as such. Wrap yourself in the wonder of who God has created you to be and then use your identity for His purposes and for His glory. You are His masterpiece!

Your specific calling and destiny are also gifts to be embraced. Delight yourself in the value of all that you have been called to accomplish this side of eternity!

The peace that God offers you in the middle of the stormy sea of demands and busy living is likewise a gift, so enjoy it! Bask in the warmth of that peace, and rest in His hope.

Your companionship with the Lord is a gift as well—so splash joyfully in your awareness of Him as you travel through life as a woman. Listen for

His reassuring voice and partner with Him in loving others, encouraging the discouraged, and offering grace to those in need.

If you ever wonder again who you are and why you are alive, remind yourself loudly and assuredly that you were created to be an image bearer of the glory of God the Father! You, dear one, are here at this moment in history to spread His unconditional love, exuberant joy, and sweet peace in the world in which you live.

Awake, awake, clothe yourself in your strength, O Zion; clothe yourself in your beautiful garments.... Shake yourself from the dust, rise up, O captive Jerusalem; loose yourself from the chains around your neck, O captive daughter of Zion. —Isaiah 52:1–2

The call for a woman to awaken to the promises and plans of God is as compelling today as it was when the prophet Isaiah first spoke these exciting words to God's people. Do you hear the sweet insistence of His voice, awakening you from your sleepy existence? He is calling you to wake up to new purpose and stretch into His plans for your one-of-a-kind life!

Do you hear the joy in God's voice as He reminds you that you are no longer covered in dust and shame, but are now clothed with glory?

He has designed an entirely new wardrobe for you to dress in. Are you not amazed by the beauty of the joy that is now yours to parade in through life? Are you not utterly astonished by the loveliness of peace that fits you so extraordinarily well? You are clothed with power from on high, and you look quite smashing in it!

You have been loosed from the chains of shame so that you are now, at last, able to freely offer life-changing encouragement and grace to those in your generation.

The Best for Last

As your sister in faith, and now as your friend, may I close with what I hope are some very practical yet compelling words of personal encouragement? Perhaps you might want to take the time to write down these assignments and keep them close at hand so that you never forget your calling, your purpose, your atmosphere, and your Companion.

+ Live each day knowing that you have been created for significance by your Creator.

+ Live each day knowing that there is a significant assignment for you to accomplish. You don't have to live a perfect life or be a perfect woman to fulfill your calling this side of heaven. Just live intentionally, joyfully, and with availability. Love those whom the Lord has placed in your pathway just for today.

+ Live each day knowing that you are not alone.

+ Live each day knowing that God's plan for your life is always surrounded by His absolute and undeniable peace.

The challenge is a simple one: live in such a way that those who come after you will thank God that you lived.

⌒

"The measure of a life, after all, is not its duration,
but its donation."
—*Corrie ten Boom*

Acknowledgments

How will I ever be able to adequately thank the tribe of family members and friends who cheer for me daily, pray for me without ceasing, and diligently spur me on in my calling?

As daunting as this task may seem…let me try!

Craig: My best friend, my life partner, my loudest cheerleader, and my husband. Other than accepting Jesus as my Lord and Savior, you are the best decision that I have ever made. Thank you for choosing me, for loving me, and for serving me. Let's do forty-two more years together!

Matthew: What a gift it has been to live close to you over the past year! I love the way you worship, the way you serve, and the way you lead. You are my son and my friend. I love having your knees under my table, your kids in my home, and your wisdom in my life. You are significant, Matt. Never doubt it.

Emily: You have become one of my dearest friends! Thank you for loving my son and for being a wonderful mom to Olivia, Wesley, Boyce, and Elizabeth Joy. You are an encourager and a woman of vibrant faith! You are significant, Emily. Never doubt it.

Christopher: It's an honor to be your mom and to have the delight of praying for you and cheering you on, even in these years when we don't see each other as often as we would like. Just know that you are loved and that you are always, always in my heart. You are significant, Christopher. Never doubt it.

Liz: Your heart to love others is amazing. Your call to serve those who need a voice is beautiful. Thank you for loving Christopher and for raising Amelia and Jack to be thoughtful, kind, and creative. Your sweet friendship is a gift to me. You are significant, Liz. Never doubt it.

Jordan: Your life is a dynamic example that God really does answer prayers. Being your mom has been one of the richest treasures of my entire life. Your talents, commitment to excellence, and creativity are a rare and compelling combination. You are significant, my miracle child. Never doubt it.

Allie: When you walked into the McLeod family, love walked in with you! You love so well, encourage without pause, and pray with purpose. Thanks for loving Jordan so well and for raising Ian to be a man of God. Your heart is pure gold in my book. You are significant, Allie. Never doubt it.

Joy: Even though you are my daughter, in this past year, you have pastored me, counseled me, and fought for me. How I love watching you and Chris love each other! I love being your mom and your friend. God is using you, dear one! You are significant, Joy. Never doubt it.

Chris: You are the son-in-law for whom I prayed for many years. What a delight that God answered my prayers with *you!* Thank you for loving Joy so well and for celebrating her. Know that I believe in you, Chris, and that I am cheering for you wildly as you tackle medical school. You are significant, Chris Barker. Never doubt it.

Joni: What a gift you were to me when I stood on the brink of forty! I loved having you around when the others had left—you became my sweet companion and kindred spirit. Now, as you walk through these young-adult years, know that I am praying for you and that I am only a phone call away. I am your mom and my heart is always turned toward you. You are significant, Joni Rebecca. Never doubt it.

Olivia: Someday you will be the one writing the books in this family! Your sweet spirit and obedient heart are a delight to everyone who knows you. I look at you and am amazed by your beauty and by your wisdom. You are so dear to me, Olivia, and I love being your Marmee.

Ian: God is going to use you, Ian, so keep close to Him all the days of your life. Your tenderness is a great strength, and your giggle is infectious! Keep reading, keep drawing, and keep dreaming. I love cheering for the Bills and for Duke with you! I love being your Marmee.

Wesley: What a spark of joy and enthusiasm you are to the McLeod family! Your insight and quest for knowledge are game-changers, for sure. Most of all, I love your tender heart and servant's ways. Can't wait to watch you in the Final Four someday! I love being your Marmee.

Amelia Grace: Keep singing your songs…keep being kind…keep dreaming…keep drinking in the life that God has given to you. I miss you every single day that we are not together. You are an amazing, girl, Amelia, and I just love being your Marmee.

Boyce: I love your perspective on faith, on prayer, and on life! You might be small, but you are mighty on the inside! Keep being the warrior that God created you to be. You are inquisitive, tenacious, and enthusiastic. What a powerful combination, indeed! I love being your Marmee.

Elizabeth Joy: I love your spunky ways, your little-girl opinions, and your joyful chatter. It's true…you do sparkle! Everything about you is captivating! You were made for greatness, dear one; don't ever forget it! I love being your Marmee.

Jack: Always remember that when you are on God's team, nothing is impossible for you, my Jack! Obey your mom and dad and enjoy being a boy! Thanks for loving Christmas with me. I love cheering for the Bills and for UNC with you and your dad! I love being your Marmee.

Mom and Leo: Thanks for loving me and for believing in me. My heart just aches to be with you, but know that I can always feel your prayers.

Nanny: Your example of godly living has inspired our entire family! Keep praying for all of us!

Norman Burton: My wonderful dad who now lives in eternity with Jesus. I wouldn't be the woman I am without having had you as my earthly father. All the credit goes to you, and all the glory goes to God.

Wesley McLeod: Craig's dad in heaven. You were the steadying force of the family McLeod. Your strength and wisdom are with us still today. See you soon!

The hardworking, generous, and incomparable staff of Carol McLeod Ministries: Angela Storm, Linda Zielinski, Danielle Stoltz, Kirsten Monroe, and Jordan McLeod. Don't we have fun together? Thanks for being my right hand, my left hand, my entire brain, and extraordinary friends. I love serving God with you.

And, of course, a special shout-out to the *Carol McLeod Ministries Board of Directors*: *Angela Storm, Kim Pickard Dudley, Sue Hilchey, Shannon Maitre, Johnnie Hampton, Tim Harner, Taci Darnelle,* and *Suzanne Kuhn.* You all are the foundation of everything that we do—thanks for being rock-solid! Thanks for steering this ship with wisdom and with passion!

John Mason: My friend and literary agent who has opened door after door after door for me! You and the Holy Spirit are a great team!

The staff at Whitaker House: Thanks for taking a chance on this persuasive, enthusiastic, and persistent author! Your friendship and your professionalism mean the world to me. I am honored and blessed to be a Whitaker House author. *Bob Whitaker, Christine Whitaker, Lois Puglisi,* and *Jim Armstrong*—you each have become so very dear to me.

LightQuest Media: Thank you for supporting me in the teaching of the Word of God through every avenue available in the twenty-first century.

Chris Busch: The words *thank you* will never be enough.

Christy Christopher: my fearless leader in prayer. When we get to heaven, we will realize the victories that you won on my behalf. I appreciate your commitment to prayer and your friendship more than words could ever express. Thank you for not being afraid of the battle!

Thank you also to the group of women who answer the desperate e-mails that come into Carol McLeod Ministries: *Linda Hoeflich, Debby Summers, Mary Buchanan,* and *Christy Christopher.* God is using you in mighty and dramatic ways! I am honored to partner with you in prayer and encouragement.

And then, to a significant team of friends who fill my life with encouragement and joy. Each one of you is a priceless gift from a loving and gracious Father:

Carolyn Hogan	*Lynn Fields*
Lisa Keller	*Debby Edwards*
Jill Janus	*Diane Phelps*
Kim Schue	*Brenda Mutton*
Kim Pickard Dudley	*Elaine Wheatley*
Susie Hilchey	*Becky Harling*
Suzanne Kuhn	*Monica Orzechowski*
Shannon Maitre	*Melissa Thompson*
Faith Blatchford	*Marilynda Lynch*
Dawn Frink	*Joy Knox*

And to *Jesus, my Lord and Savior.* Thank You for calling me, equipping me, anointing me, and choosing me for Your grand purposes. I live to make hell smaller and heaven bigger! I live to honor You with every breath, with every word, and with every minute of my life!

About the Author

Carol McLeod is a popular speaker at women's conferences and retreats through Carol McLeod Ministries. She is the author of eleven books, including *StormProof* (Whitaker House, 2019), *Guide Your Mind, Guard Your Heart, Grace Your Tongue* (Whitaker House, 2018), *Joy for All Seasons* (Bridge-Logos, 2016), *Holy Estrogen* (Harrison House, 2012), and *Defiant Joy* (Thomas Nelson, 2006). Carol hosts a daily podcast, *A Jolt of Joy!* on the Charisma Podcast Network, and a weekly podcast, *The Joy of Motherhood*, which is listened to by thousands of moms around the world. Her blog, *Joy for the Journey* (formerly *A Cup of Tea with Carol*), has been named in the Top 50 Faith Blogs for Women. After her 2013 devotional *21 Days to Beat Depression* had nearly 100,000 downloads in the first month, YouVersion picked it up, where it has been read over 500,000 times in five years. She also has twelve other devotionals on YouVersion, including *Guide Your Mind, Guard Your Heart, Grace Your Tongue; StormProof;* and *Significant Destiny.* Carol writes a weekly column for *Ministry Today* and often writes for *Charisma* magazine. She is also a frequent guest on and has cohosted *100 Huntley Street.* Her teaching DVD *The Rooms of a Woman's Heart* won a Telly Award in 2005 for excellence in religious programming. Carol was also the first Women's Chaplain at Oral Roberts University.

Carol has been married to her college sweetheart, Craig, for over forty years and is the mother of five children in heaven and five children on earth. Carol and Craig are now enjoying their new titles as "Marmee and Pa" to seven captivating grandchildren! She and her husband recently moved to Oklahoma, where Craig serves as the North American Director for Global Partners, a missions organization that plants churches in remote areas of the world.